Cambridge Elements

Elements in Modern Wars

THE LEAGUE OF NATIONS

Joseph Maiolo
King's College London

Laura Robson
Yale University

CAMBRIDGE
UNIVERSITY PRESS

Shaftesbury Road, Cambridge CB2 8EA, United Kingdom

One Liberty Plaza, 20th Floor, New York, NY 10006, USA

477 Williamstown Road, Port Melbourne, VIC 3207, Australia

314–321, 3rd Floor, Plot 3, Splendor Forum, Jasola District Centre, New Delhi – 110025, India

103 Penang Road, #05–06/07, Visioncrest Commercial, Singapore 238467

Cambridge University Press is part of Cambridge University Press & Assessment, a department of the University of Cambridge.

We share the University's mission to contribute to society through the pursuit of education, learning and research at the highest international levels of excellence.

www.cambridge.org
Information on this title: www.cambridge.org/9781009514156

DOI: 10.1017/9781009514149

© Joseph Maiolo and Laura Robson 2025

This publication is in copyright. Subject to statutory exception and to the provisions of relevant collective licensing agreements, with the exception of the Creative Commons version the link for which is provided below, no reproduction of any part may take place without the written permission of Cambridge University Press & Assessment.

An online version of this work is published at doi.org/10.1017/9781009514149 under a Creative Commons Open Access license CC-BY-NC 4.0 which permits re-use, distribution and reproduction in any medium for non-commercial purposes providing appropriate credit to the original work is given and any changes made are indicated. To view a copy of this license visit https://creativecommons.org/licenses/by-nc/4.0

When citing this work, please include a reference to the DOI 10.1017/9781009514149

First published 2025

A catalogue record for this publication is available from the British Library

ISBN 978-1-009-51415-6 Hardback
ISBN 978-1-009-51412-5 Paperback
ISSN 2633-8378 (online)
ISSN 2633-836X (print)

Cambridge University Press & Assessment has no responsibility for the persistence or accuracy of URLs for external or third-party internet websites referred to in this publication and does not guarantee that any content on such websites is, or will remain, accurate or appropriate.

The League of Nations

Elements in Modern Wars

DOI: 10.1017/9781009514149
First published online: January 2025

Joseph Maiolo
King's College London

Laura Robson
Yale University

Authors for correspondence: Joseph Maiolo, joe.maiolo@kcl.ac.uk, Laura Robson, laura.robson@yale.edu

Abstract: The Element challenges histories of the League of Nations that present it as a meaningful if flawed experiment in global governance. Such accounts have largely failed to admit its overriding purpose: not to work towards international cooperation among equally sovereign states, but to claim control over the globe's resources, weapons, and populations for its main showrunners (including the United States) – and not through the gentle arts of persuasion and negotiation but through the direct and indirect use of force and the monopolization of global military and economic power. The League's advocates framed its innovations, from refugee aid to disarmament, as manifestations of its commitment to an obvious universal good and, often, as a series of technocratic, scientific solutions to the problems of global disorder. But its practices shored up the dominance of the Western victors and preserved long-standing structures of international power and civilizational–racial hierarchy. This title is also available as Open Access on Cambridge Core.

Keywords: League of Nations, international order, empire, humanitarianism, disarmament

© Joseph Maiolo and Laura Robson 2025

ISBNs: 9781009514156 (HB), 9781009514125 (PB), 9781009514149 (OC)
ISSNs: 2633-8378 (online), 2633-836X (print)

Contents

Introduction: The Idea of International Order   1

1 Ordering People   22

2 Ordering Wealth   44

3 Ordering War   69

Epilogue: The Means and Ends of the League of Nations   91

Introduction: The Idea of International Order

'The league will have to occupy the great position which has been rendered vacant by the destruction of so many of the old European empires and the passing away of the old European order.'
Jan Smuts, *The League of Nations: A Practical Suggestion*

'It should be remembered that the members of the Secretariat are not representative of their countries. They are there solely as experts in law, economics, history and administrative problems. So they can and do approach problems with a scientific detachment which is novel in international affairs.'
Sarah Wambaugh, 'A New Kind of Frontier', 1923

A first great experiment in international governance? A noble if abortive attempt to keep the peace in Europe? An unwitting but effective generator of new anticolonial pressures and decolonial sovereignties? Historians in recent years have placed the long-neglected League of Nations under a microscope, seeing in it the seeds of a postcolonial world order and a meaningful if flawed experiment in the mechanics of modern international political authority. The League now enjoys the reputation of a grand, but defeated, enterprise: one whose goals of maintaining the peace and preserving a new, semi-imperial economic and political stability ran up against unresolvable local, regional, and global contradictions, and eventually faltered altogether in the face of the simultaneous rise of Nazism and fascism. This League failed in its peace-making endeavours, but opened up new arenas of objection to empire, global economic cooperation, and international coordination of everything from currency stabilization to refugee aid. In this interpretation, the League – sometimes despite itself – acted as midwife in the birth of a modern era in which postcolonial sovereignties, human rights, and principles of international cooperation would enjoy a much-enhanced though never unchallenged status.

Such accounts have broadly failed to admit the League's own overriding purpose. This was not to work towards international cooperation among equally sovereign states, or to promote economic stability in a shattered post-war Europe, or to ensure new forms of global security and prosperity. Rather, it was to claim control over the world's resources, war-making potential, and populations for the League's main showrunners – and not through the gentle arts of persuasion, collaboration, and negotiation but through the direct and indirect use of physical force and the monopolization of global military and economic power. The League's advocates framed its structural and political innovations, from refugee aid to global labour regulation to disarmament, as manifestations of its evident commitment to an obvious universal good. But upon close

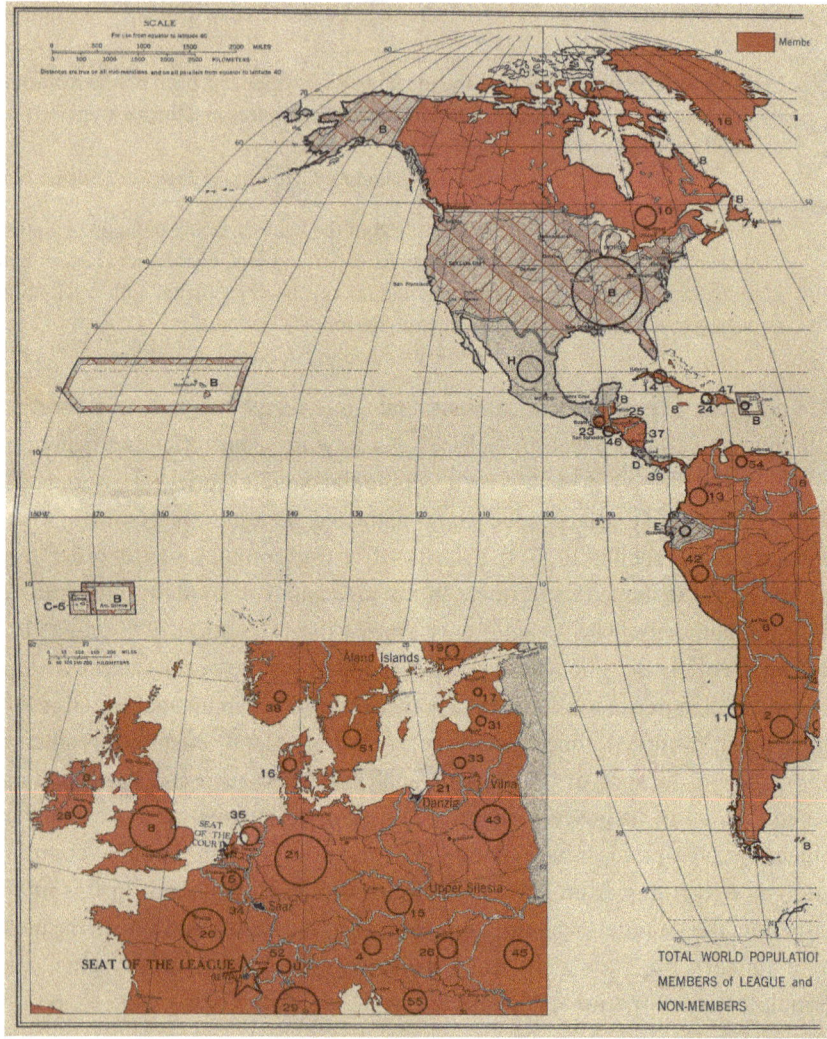

Figure 1a Expansive vision of the global reach of the League of Nations, made by geographer Laura Martin (1884–1956), an expert on legal issues relating to sovereignty in Antarctica, in 1925/27. League of Nations Archives.

examination all its practices pointed to the same goal: shoring up the dominance of the Western victors and preserving the structures of international power and the civilizational-racial hierarchies that had long sustained them, now in a form that could survive the fall of formal empire. In other words, the League of Nations was an experiment not in international governance but in the production, maintenance, and extension of imperially derived geopolitical hierarchies: organized around race, claiming near-total monopolies on wealth, and backed

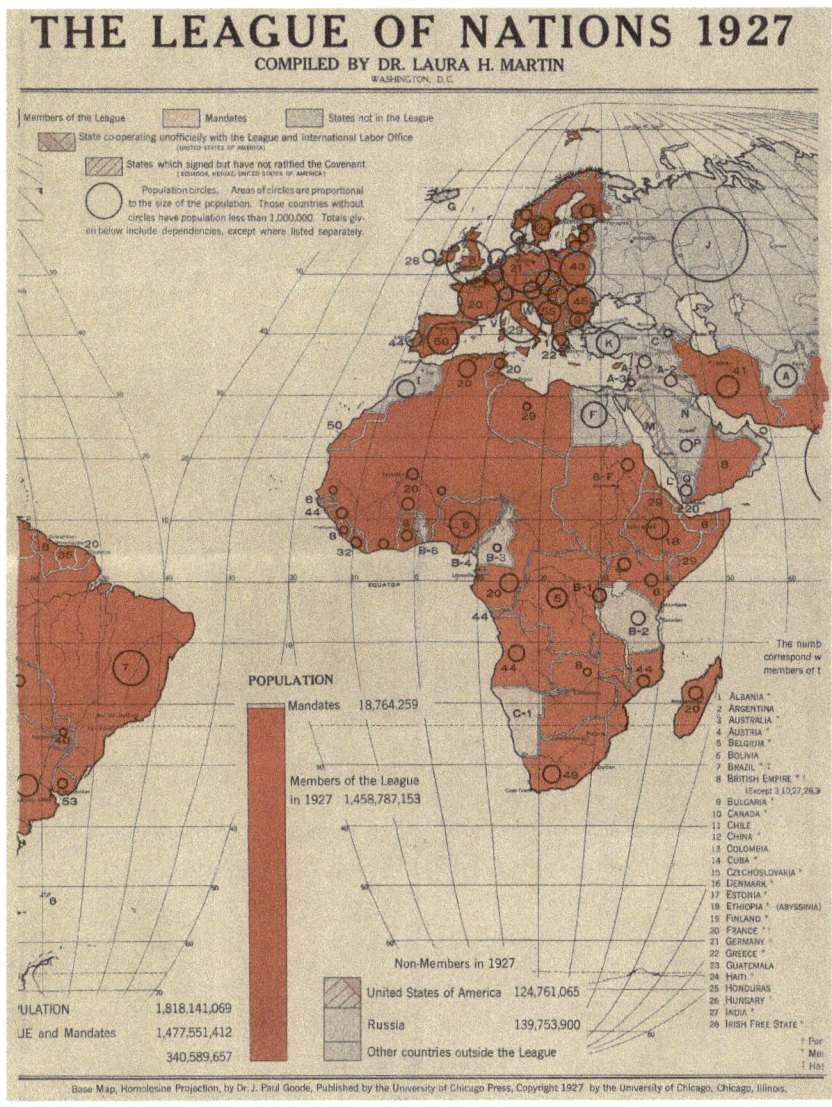

Figure 1b (cont.)

by overwhelming military supremacy and the perpetual threat (and not infrequently actual use) of physical violence.

This study seeks to outline the origins, philosophies, and practices of League from its inception to its dissolution, from two different perspectives: the bottom-up encounter with this forcible ordering of people and wealth experienced by colonial subjects and economically or politically subjugated regions of the post-war world on the one hand, and the top-down strategic view of 'peace-making'

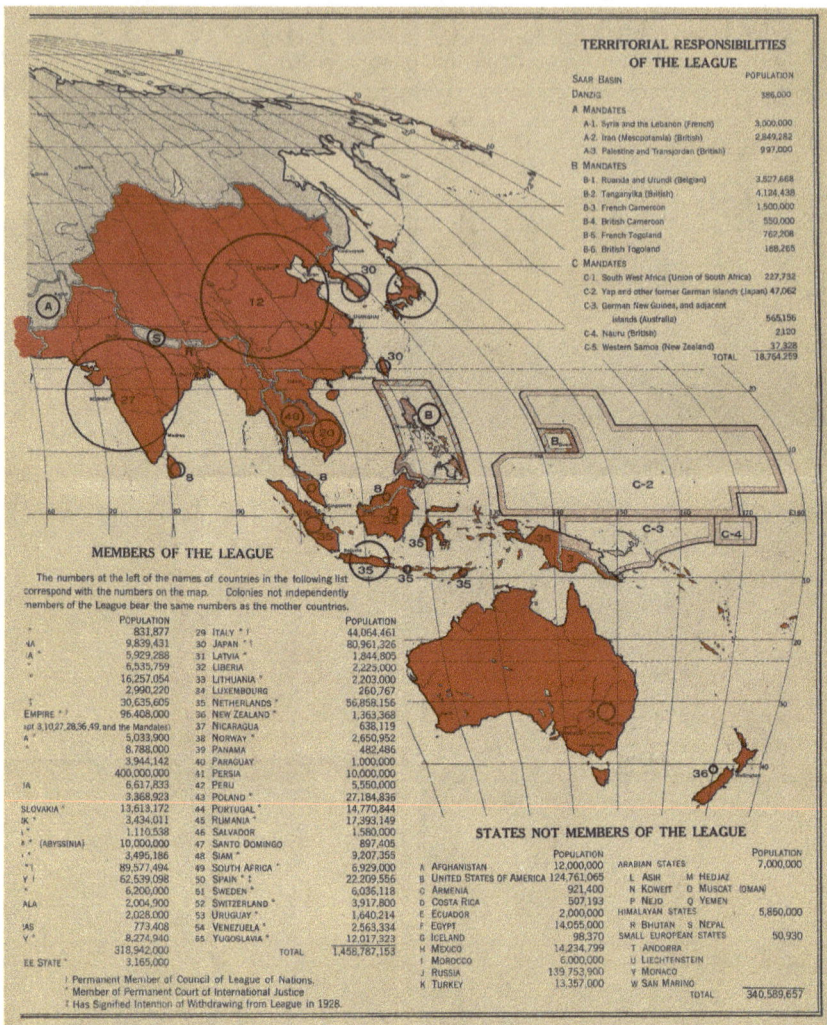

Figure 1c (cont.)

promulgated and institutionalized by its main (imperial) architects on the other. Its section order – People, Wealth, and War – reverses that of conventional treatments that view the League chiefly as an instrument for ending the First World War, and reflects a different understanding of the League as a colonial, imperial, and power-political enterprise. Taken together, these dual experiences of the League's words and practice clearly indicated its primary reason for being: to order the world according to the (always contested and shifting) economic and political interests of its great-power sponsors and beneficiaries, including the United States.

Such a liberal imperial ordering of the world's people and resources could – indeed, had to – be presented as a natural one, emerging uncontested out of the post-war era's rule of experts and representing a neutral, scientific approach to the problems of global governance. Much of the League's practice, then, was taken up with the active and conscious process of removing discussion from the realm of the public into the realm of incontestable forms of technical expertise – an approach that naturalized imperial hierarchy as scientific, and painted the myriad political objections to Allied agglomerations of power and resources, coming from all sorts of quarters, as mere ignorance or ineptitude. These rhetorical and procedural devices removed discussion of the League's economic and political reordering of its realms from the dangers of public opinion; but, of course, they did not solve the problem of enforcement, which had to come from elsewhere – in the event, from the continued projection of ex-Allied military power into colonial and semi-colonial territories. The brutalities of the mandates system in the Middle East represented only one aspect of the violence and threat of violence that characterized the imposition of League-supported visions of order across the globe, from China to Africa to Latin America to Eastern Europe.

The League and Its Reception

The League of Nations was the first global institution tasked with organizing international relations and shaping world order (see Figures 1a–c & 2). It was established at the Paris Peace Conference of 1919, held its first meetings in Geneva in 1920, and was disbanded on 18 April 1946, when it turned its buildings, assets, and archives over to its successor, the United Nations.

The League consisted of the Assembly, the Council, the Secretariat, and, from 1921, the Permanent Court of Justice (see Figure 3). The Assembly was a public forum for debate among the delegates of all member states, each of which had one vote on issues like the admission of new members and appointments to the Permanent Court of Justice. It also functioned as an advisory body on changes to international treaties, and oversaw the work of the Council and the League's technical committees. The Council consisted of the most powerful members of the organization (initially Britain, France, Italy, and Japan) and a few additional non-permanent members. As the League's top decision-making body, the Council deliberated on international disputes, acted on the recommendations of the Assembly, and nominated the secretary general. The Secretariat, as we shall see, was not simply a sprawling network of hundreds of administrators who ran the day-to-day affairs of the institution, but a diplomatic machine exerting influence across a broad range of political domains (colonial mandates, minorities, armaments, the world economy,

Figure 2 League of Nations Building, New York World's Fair, July 1939. League of Nations Archives.

cultural exchange, healthcare) through the dissemination of internationally legitimized knowledge and the application of technocratic expertise.[1] The same can be said of what was arguably the League's most important additional agency, the International Labour Organisation (ILO), which drew on the expertise of the international socialist movement to promote social reforms through the promulgation of standards and regulations concerning such issues as working hours, child labour, and the employment of refugees.[2] Several other agencies claimed similar kinds of expert, scientific approaches: the Health Organisation, the International Commission on Intellectual Cooperation, the Permanent Central Opium Board, the High Commission for Refugees, and the Economic and Financial Organization.

---

[1] Karen Gram-Skjoldager and Haakon A. Ikonomou, 'Making Sense of the League of Nations Secretariat – Historiographical and Conceptual Reflections on Early International Public Administration', *European History Quarterly* 49/3 (2019), 420–44.

[2] Sandrine Kott and Joëlle Droux, eds., *Globalizing Social Rights: The International Labour Organization and Beyond* (London: Palgrave, 2013).

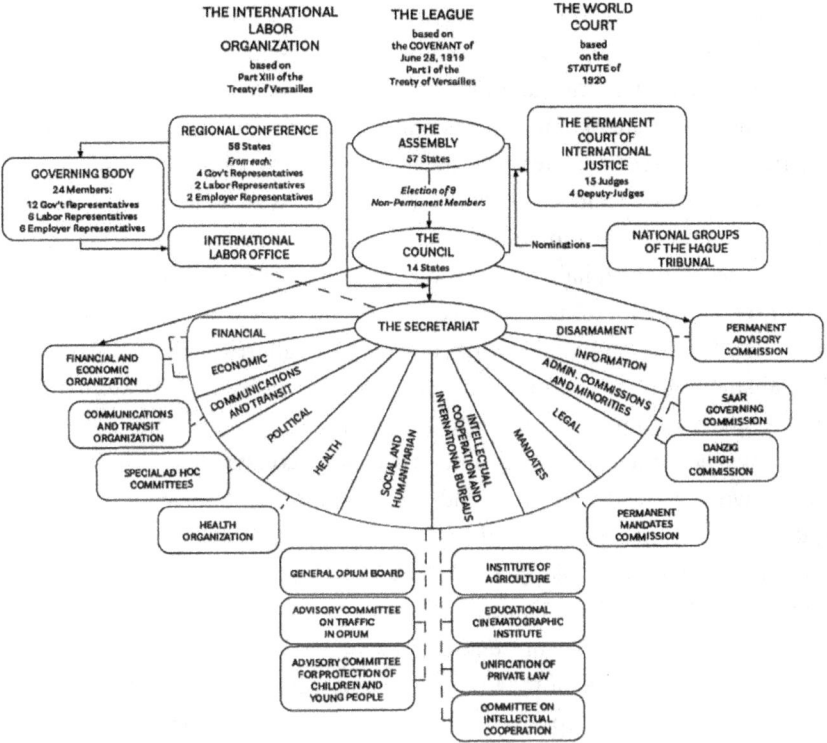

Figure 3 Organizational structure of the League of Nations. Diagram by Tam Rankin.

Legally, the League came into existence with the signing of the Treaty of Versailles on 28 June 1919 – underscoring the link between the outcomes of the First World War and the creation of a new institution intended to enshrine a postwar geopolitical *status quo*. Its Covenant consisted of twenty-six articles: seven establishing the rules and structure of the League, thirteen setting out its role in disarmament, collective security and international arbitration, and six recognizing the Monroe Doctrine (US dominance in the western hemisphere) and proposing principles of governance for colonial 'mandates', national minorities, and cooperation with the International Red Cross. Membership in the League was voluntary, though Germany was excluded until 1926. Over the lifetime of the League, sixty-two recognized sovereign states became members at one time or another; in 1937–38 it still had fifty-three active members.

Over the course of the past century, interpretations of the League have gone, very broadly speaking, from boosterism to condemnation to a kind of attenuated enthusiasm. In the hopeful but psychologically difficult terrain of the early 1920s, Western descriptions of the League featured buoyant narratives about its pacific possibilities and its utopian visions. (Soviet sources, equally reflective of their own political context, viewed it mainly as an extension of nineteenth-century British and French imperial expansion.) During periods of time when the outlook for what liberal observers thought of as cooperative internationalism seemed bleak – in the run-up to the Second World War and then again through the Cold War years – the League was broadly condemned as a failure. In the post–Cold War era of unipolarity and a sense of the permanent triumph of liberal capitalism – Francis Fukuyama's 'end of history' – it once again transformed into an inventive, promising, and at least semi-successful gambit. More recently, following the myriad failures and humiliations of liberalism from the 'war on terror' forward, specialized works from various quarters have begun to reconsider this position, seeing in the League something distinctly more menacing. It is time, perhaps, to collate some of this contemporary work into a broader reconsideration of the intent, meaning, and consequences of this first experiment in global governance – with an awareness of the ways in which both scholarly and popular interpretations of the League's role, actions, and legacies have tended to serve not just as evaluations of the past but also as assessments of the present.

The earliest accounts of the League, coming particularly from legal scholars interested in emerging concepts of internationalism (and including not a few who had themselves participated in the League's construction or early operations), tended to emphasize its stated ideological commitment to global peace and stability and its initial successes in 'technical' realms like refugee resettlement, currency stabilization, and the distribution of raw materials. But following the League's dissolution in the late 1930s and the advent of an even more catastrophic global war, scholarly enthusiasm for the League died down. The few works produced on the League in the aftermath of the Second World War tended, as one historian has put it, to represent '"decline and fall" narratives or analytical postmortems' – painting a picture of its tragic descent, in just a few decades, from high hopes and higher ideals to disillusionment and collapse.[3] In the aftermath of the Soviet Union's disintegration and the end of the Cold War, though, a new and explicitly revisionist narrative began to dispute this apparently long-settled story about the 'failures' of the League of Nations. Now, international historians searching for histories of (and, perhaps, models for) global institution-building in this brave new unipolar world of hyper-globalization and liberalization began to see the League in a new light: not as a failure but as a useful, interesting, and innovative experiment, one whose

---

[3] Susan Pedersen, 'Back to the League of Nations', *American Historical Review* 112/4 (2007), 1091–117.

successes were as real as its disappointments and whose enduring influence had long been underrated or misunderstood. As historian Susan Pedersen put it in an influential 2007 essay,

> if these League systems could not coerce states or override sovereignty, they did contribute powerfully to the articulation and diffusion of international norms, some of which proved lasting... The League was the training ground for these men and women – the place where they learned skills, built alliances, and began to craft that fragile network of norms and agreement by which our world is regulated, if not quite governed.[4]

Pedersen was one of several prominent scholars who, if they retained some of the critiques of the previous generation, nevertheless saw much to like in the League. Akira Iriye's 2002 book *Global Community* understood post-1919 internationalism as an essentially cooperative endeavour, interrupted rather than prompted by the war and bringing an ideology of global cooperation to an otherwise brutal interstate system during the interwar period. 'International institutions, both governmental and nongovernmental,' he wrote, 'represented the conscience of the world when individual states were destroying the peace... Global consciousness was kept alive by the heroic efforts of nonstate actors that preserved the vision of one world.'[5] While not quite so unreservedly complimentary, Patricia Clavin's 2013 book *Securing the World Economy*, on the League's Economic and Financial Organization, likewise understood League-led internationalism to have made notable strides towards an integrated world. 'The multiplicity of activities and perspectives frequently rendered the whole League ineffective in an international crisis,' she wrote,

> yet it simultaneously meant that, out of the diversity of its responses, information was exchanged, and national positions clarified in a process that, over time, opened up the possibility for different outcomes in the future. It also allowed for fruitful connections to be made across spheres, such as economics and health, or finance and security, which may have been impeded by the creation of discrete institutions.[6]

Both these authors noted especially the League's commitment to and successes in arenas of 'technical' knowledge and information-sharing across borders: reconstruction, food provision and distribution, labour controls, health initiatives, to name a few. In such readings, if the League had failed to bring 'security', it had nevertheless promoted international cooperation in ways that

---

[4] Pedersen, 'Back to the League of Nations', 1116.
[5] Akira Iriye, *Global Community: The Role of International Organizations in the Making of the Contemporary World* (Berkeley: University of California, 2004), 36.
[6] Patricia Clavin, *Securing the World Economy: The Reinvention of the League of Nations* (Oxford: Oxford University Press, 2013), 5.

presaged positive aspects of the internationalisms of our own era. As Glenda Sluga, Peter Jackson, and William Mulligan put it in perhaps the most recent restatement of these arguments, 'The UN, European integration, decolonization, greater popular participation in international politics, the codification of international law and the restraints on power politics had their roots in the possibilities of peacemaking after the First World War.'[7]

In her book-length exploration, Pedersen even managed to bring such arguments to one of the most-reviled aspects of the League: the mandates system. *The Guardians: The League of Nations and the Crisis of Empire* represented the first history of the Permanent Mandates Commission (PMC), the League's governing body for its colonies-lite system under which certain of the Allied powers were issued responsibility for the administration of ex-Ottoman and ex-German colonial territories 'inhabited by peoples not yet able to stand by themselves under the strenuous conditions of the modern world', as the infamous Article 22 of the League Covenant put it. While acknowledging the colonial nature of the mandatory system and its promotion of racial hierarchies of civilization and sovereignty, Pedersen nevertheless viewed the PMC as a site of productive internationalist discourse that wrought more than it intended. 'The mandate system,' she wrote, 'opened up imperial rule to an uncontainable wave of scrutiny and "talk" ... the League, against its own desires and intentions, helped to bring the European empires down.'[8] In this reading, the League's pledges to ensure public review and discussion of its actions collided with its basic commitment to empire, opening up the mandates to global critique of a sort that eventually managed to bring the whole system into question and created a new international landscape inclusive of newly decolonial sovereign states.

Such revisionist arguments did not go unchallenged for long. One critic, the influential historian of Europe and the Balkans Mark Mazower, staked out an at least half-sceptical position in his 2012 book *Governing the World*: a work that repeated shibboleths about the success of the League's 'technical' work, but also offered a sharp critique of the idea that the organization somehow inadvertently opened the doors to imperial dissolution. 'In a small way, perhaps, by establishing the principle of international oversight and making it respectable,' he noted, 'the commission paved the way for post-war decolonization. But it is worth asking how long the colonies might have remained under imperial or mandatory rule had the Second World War not intervened and American

---

[7] Peter Jackson, William Mulligan, and Glenda Sluga, 'Introduction', in Peter Jackson, William Mulligan, and Glenda Sluga, eds., *Peacemaking and International Order after the First World War* (Cambridge: Cambridge University Press, 2023), 1–34.

[8] Susan Pedersen, *The Guardians: The League of Nations and the Crisis of Empire* (New York: Oxford University Press, 2017), 406.

anticolonialism (and America's fear of Bolshevism) not been added to the mix.'⁹ The idea that the League could, even unwittingly, be an agent of any kind of liberation was met with even greater scepticism among scholars whose work was based in the regions that had found themselves under mandatory rule, most notably the Middle East and Africa. The 2015 *Routledge Handbook of the Middle Eastern Mandates*, co-edited by historians Andrew Arsan and Cyrus Schayegh and conceived as an update to a similar 2004 collection by Peter Sluglett and Nadine Méouchy, depicted the mandates not just as a continuation but an extension, both geographical and territorial, of old and brutal forms of racial empire.¹⁰ Similarly, recent scholarship on Africa has not, by and large, been willing to accept the rosier conclusions of Europeanists like Pedersen vis-à-vis the liberationist possibilities of the mandate system or (by extension) the League. As Molly McCullers has recently put it with reference to mandatory Namibia, histories from the perspective of the colonized put paid to the idea that the mandate system opened a path to decolonization despite itself, instead illustrating mainly 'how the mandates' purposeful indeterminacy could delay a territory's rite of passage from colony to nation-state and indefinitely extend its liminality'.¹¹

The most recent assessments of interwar internationalism, perhaps reflecting a greater distance from the triumphalism of the post–Cold War years and a rather more pessimistic view of the longer-term ramifications of an untrammelled global neoliberalism, have begun to suggest that the League – and in particular its economic policies – was mainly concerned with protecting the principle of private property and controlling the international distribution of labour rather than the promotion of world peace and international security.¹² This is especially true of economic historians who have cast a critical eye on the machinations of twentieth-century global capitalism, and of more semiotic approaches that understand the League as (in Carolyn Biltoft's words) 'a truth and symbolic capital production system'.¹³ Still, even this recent literature has often retained the old

---

⁹ Mark Mazower, *Governing the World: The History of an Idea* (New York: Penguin, 2013), 170.
¹⁰ Andrew Arsan and Cyrus Schayegh, eds., *The Routledge Handbook of the History of the Middle East Mandates* (London: Routledge, 2015), and Nadine Méouchy and Peter Sluglett, eds., *The British and French Mandates in Comparative Perspectives* (Leiden: Brill, 2004).
¹¹ Molly McCullers, 'Betwixt and between Colony and Nation-State: Liminality, Decolonization, and the South West Africa Mandate', *American Historical Review* 124/5 (2019), 1704–08. Similar arguments vis-à-vis other African mandates can be found in George Njung, Benjamin Lawrance, and Meredith Terreta in their contributions to the same issue.
¹² For instance: Quinn Slobodian, *The Globalists: The End of Empire and the Birth of Neoliberalism* (Cambridge, MA: Harvard University Press, 2018), and Nicolas Mulder, *The Economic Weapon: The Rise of Sanctions as a Tool of Modern War* (New Haven: Yale University Press, 2022).
¹³ See Clara Mattei, *The Capital Order: How Economist Invented Austerity and Paved the Way to Fascism* (Chicago: University of Chicago Press, 2022). Carolyn Biltoft 's *A Violent Peace:*

commitment to the idea of international order as a self-evident good, and continues to single out the League's 'technical' bodies for approbation even while acknowledging the long-term consequences of the League's neo-imperial practices. Historian Sandrine Kott's notes on the ILO represent a good example: while she acknowledges 'a fundamental tension... between the promise of social justice and the decommodification of labour that this promise embodies and its role as a social agent of economic globalisation', she also takes note of its 'normative work, based on a skilful exchange of ideas between ILO officials and those of national administrations, [that] enabled the establishment of a recognised social expertise and know-how' – norms that remain 'important reference points even when they are not ratified'.[14]

One of the questions that a history of the League brings up, then, is: Should we understand the effort to build a liberal internationalism, in itself, as a worthy goal aimed at the creation of a more secure and just world? Historians have tended to think the answer is yes; as Mark Mazower has put it, 'their guiding assumption seems to be that the emergence of some kind of global community is not only desirable but inevitable'.[15] While often decrying the severely punitive elements designed to hold Germany and its allies accountable, historians' assessments routinely balance this punitive impulse with what they see as a positive attempt to transcend the war-prone anarchy of pre-1914 imperialism by organizing peace and 'security' in the form of the League. Within the universe of historians, Waqaf Zaidi's assertion that such 'security' was built mainly to guarantee 'the ongoing subjugation of [the Allies'] enemies' represents an outlier position[16] – one more in line with political scientists, who have often answered this question rather differently. From this disciplinary perspective, it is more common to consider international order building to be at best normatively neutral and in any case profoundly implicated in the maintenance of imperially derived geopolitical hierarchies. The work of scholars like Lora Anne Viola and Kyle Lascurettes suggests that after great wars emerging hegemons do not generally seek to make their rule acceptable to other states by constructing inclusive world orders; instead, they establish 'exclusive orders' to inhibit the emergence of future

---

Media, Truth, and Power at the League of Nations (Chicago: University of Chicago Press, 2021) constitutes an unusual and idiosyncratic attempt to think through the connections between 'mass media, mass markets, and mass violence'.

[14] Sandrine Kott, 'ILO: Social Justice in a Global World? A History in Tension', *International Development Policy: Revue internationale de politique de développement* 11 (2019), 21–39. https://doi.org/10.4000/poldev.2991.

[15] Mark Mazower, *No Enchanted Palace: The End of Empire and the Ideological Origins of the United Nations* (Princeton: Princeton University Press, 2009), 5.

[16] Waqaf Zaidi, *Technological Internationalism and World Order* (Cambridge: Cambridge University Press, 2021), 13.

great power threats.[17] The overriding logic of ordering is thus competition, exclusion, and stratification – precisely what we can see emerging from the post-war negotiations from 1919 and in the construction of the League itself.

If, then, the current literature features a still-dominant view that the League represented a sphere for 'progress' – albeit an incomplete and politically compromised version – it also includes a number of more critical (and, often, more locally specific) takes on the League as a complicated and temporary but nevertheless insidious, effective, and influential agent of empire and its attendant radical inequalities. It is with this historiographical tension in mind that we will begin our own explorations.

Long-Term Origins

The League of Nations had two major points of origin, both centred on 'great power' interests: nineteenth-century British and French imperial practice, translated for a new global audience and adjusted to accommodate shifting discursive norms, and a more immediate set of wartime imperatives for the preservation of the liberal empires in a moment of global conflagration.

Internationalism as both idea and practice had deep roots in the nineteenth century: not only in the imperial agreements and carve-ups emerging from the Congress of Vienna and its many later iterations, but also in the emergence of non-governmental institutions that appeared humanitarian or pacifist but in fact were designed to support ever more expansive applications of imperial rule. 'International' cooperation in the form of distribution of territory among empires found its most explicit moment in the Berlin Congress of 1884, which in its unabashed handing-out of African land to the European empires arguably prefigured the League's parcelling out of former Ottoman and German territories to the Allied powers; certainly, the concept of a European concert underpinned the idea of the League. But there were other, less overtly political actors involved as well, who were collectively transforming the exercise of nineteenth-century empire into an all-inclusive internationalist practice. Some had to do with negotiations over cross-border communications, like the International Telegraphic Union (established in 1865) and the Universal Postal Union (1874). Others had more explicitly to do with the nature and conduct of war: most notably perhaps the International Committee of Red Cross, established in 1863 by international treaty and embedded at the national level in military and especially army practice. Health, too, became a venue for

---

[17] Lora Anne Viola, *The Closure of the International System: How Institutions Create Political Equalities and Hierarchies* (Cambridge: Cambridge University Press, 2020); Kyle Lascurettes, *Orders of Exclusion: Great Powers and the Strategic Sources of Foundational Rules in International Relations* (Oxford: Oxford University Press, 2020).

international cooperation through such new organizations as the International Central Bureau for the Campaign against Tuberculosis.[18] All these theoretically non-political enterprises were deeply engaged with national governments, and they all provided imperial venues for the active and ongoing negotiation of local and regional conditions in the run-up to the First World War, as the window for claiming new territory appeared to be closing. Such organizations assumed the possibility of regulating conditions of conflict from a supranational stance, approved and moderated by states themselves. In other words, these collaborations in the realms of communications, cultural exchange, health, and the rules of war all sought to stabilize the imperial system by producing limited but meaningful venues for the negotiation and pre-emption of potentially clashing imperial claims through external controls on local conditions.

In addition, the late nineteenth century saw the major European empires increasingly encouraging, and sometimes actively constructing, communalism and nationalism as spheres for various forms of 'internationalist' intervention. Philo-Hellenic associations supporting Greek resistance to the Ottomans and the construction of a territorially ambitious Greek state, for instance, positioned Western European Christian support for Greek separatism as a kind of internationalist cause tied to liberal political commitments. Many observers on the ground noted that such interventions, tagged as liberationist and internationalist, in fact often served to stoke the kind of local, intercommunal violence that would eventually produce highly exclusionary forms of nationalism and render multinational communities untenable; but they served the cause of empire in their production of ragged, weak separatist states that needed Western European imperial backing to survive.[19] Similarly, the Berlin Conference's positioning of the Ottoman treatment of its Armenian communities as a site for international monitoring and if necessary intervention served primarily not to benefit Armenian communities themselves (whose position in the empire was in fact substantially damaged by this imperial association) but to provide Britain and France with a legitimization of political, military, and commercial intervention in the Ottoman sphere, particularly against Russian interests.[20] Even the Red Cross, so apparently humanitarian in its purpose and operations, arguably

---

[18] See Iriye, *Global Community*, and Sakiko Kaiga, *Britain and the Intellectual Origins of the League of Nations, 1914–1919* (Cambridge: Cambridge University Press, 2021), especially chapter 1.

[19] This is a point that Ottomanists have developed very thoroughly, particularly with reference to the late nineteenth-century Balkans. See, for instance, Benjamin C. Fortna, Stefanos Katsikas, Dimitris Kamouzis, and Paraskevas Konortas, eds., *State-Nationalism in the Ottoman Empire, Greece and Turkey: Orthodox and Muslims, 1830–1945* (London: Routledge, 2013), and Ipek Yosmaoglu, *Blood Ties: Religion, Violence, and the Politics of Nationhood in Ottoman Macedonia, 1878–1908* (Ithaca: Cornell University Press, 2014), among others.

[20] See, for instance, Bedross Matossian, *The Horrors of Adana: Revolution and Violence in the Early Twentieth Century* (Stanford: Stanford University Press, 2022).

smoothed the path for imperial violence – perhaps particularly in the Balkans – by assuming the basic legitimacy of contemporary forms of bloodshed, and assuring an anxious metropolitan public of the active mitigation of their most brutal aspects.[21] (On this point, it is perhaps worth noting the concentration of such relief schemes in areas of conflict where the concept of 'rules of war' were broadly agreed not to apply.[22])

The League would also draw heavily on one of the crucial concepts of nineteenth-century empire: extraterritoriality. Developed with special reference to spaces of informal imperial influence, notably China and the Ottoman Empire, ideas about the creation and enforcement of special spheres of economic, political, and military operation would become central to the League's conception of its own role and the exemptions it was providing to its primary showrunners. In the Ottoman sphere, the role of the so-called capitulations treaties – agreements exempting foreigners from adherence to Ottoman law and taxation, dating from the seventeenth century and by 1914 one of the most reviled aspects of the Ottoman–European relationship – was recast by Britain, France, and the League in the mandate texts to ensure the continuation of the previous era's commercial privileges for European firms operating in the Levant. Nineteenth-century practices around the capitulations also provided a model for how to cast 'minority rights' as a legitimate internationalist site of concern and action in semi-colonial areas of the world.[23] Debt, too, persisted as a venue for intervention; the League's enforcement of repayment terms for imperial debts offered a liberal rationale for a continued imperial presence across the Middle East and Asia that clearly recalled nineteenth-century British and French practice in places like Egypt.[24]

Short-Term Origins

All these precedents enjoyed a renewed relevance with the rise of new forms of Allied cooperation, particularly with respect to money and raw materials,

---

[21] Davide Rodogno, *Night on Earth: A History of International Humanitarianism in the Near East, 1918–1930* (Cambridge: Cambridge University Press, 2022).

[22] See especially Samuel Moyn, *Humane: How the United States Abandoned Peace and Reinvented War* (New York: Farrar, Straus and Giroux, 2021); Priya Satia, 'The Defense of Inhumanity: Air Control and the British Idea of Arabia', American Historical Review 111/1 (2006), 16–51; and Martin Thomas, *Violence and the Colonial Order: Police, Workers, and Protest in the European Colonial Empires, 1918–1940* (Cambridge: Cambridge University Press, 2012).

[23] Laura Robson, 'Capitulations Redux: The Imperial Genealogy of the Post-World War I "Minority" Regimes', *American Historical Review* 126/3 (2021), 978–1000.

[24] Mustafa Aksakal and Patrick Schilling, 'Turkey and the Division of the Ottoman Debt at Lausanne ', in Jonathan Conlin and Ozan Ozavci, eds., *They All Made Peace – What Is Peace? The 1923 Lausanne Treaty and the New Imperial Order* (London: Gingko, 2023), 235–58.

during the First World War. As early as 1915, the Allied representatives were discussing economic cooperation as a basis of their collective military effort – as Lloyd George put it, constructing 'not only an alliance of military forces, but an alliance of financial forces'.[25] Historian Jamie Martin has traced the development of large-scale forms of wartime cooperation around the acquisition of raw materials, from the early establishment of the Commission Internationale de Ravitaillement (International Resupplying Commission) in 1914 through a series of agreements on wheat prices in the middle part of the war to the eventual emergence of the Allied Maritime Transport Council, which included the United States in its organization of imports and pricing vis-à-vis the Allied powers.[26] This sort of inter-imperial cooperation, eventually encompassing the United States as well as the Entente, was from its inception viewed as a potential model for post-war cooperation with an eye to permanent Allied hegemony.

In all these cases, concerns about scarcity mobilized Allied officials to look for collective and collaborative ways to guarantee access, at the lowest possible cost, to all the raw materials necessary for the continuation of the war, from minerals to foodstuffs to fuel. Indeed, it was worries about shortages that led to early proposals that the League should have the power to engage in economic sanctioning to protect access to raw materials and thereby ensure the full employment necessary for post-war stability.[27] But as the war drew to a close, it gradually became clear that the real issue for the surviving empires (including the United States) was not scarcity but the spectre of overproduction and price collapse. Over the coming years, then, the League would recommit to the concept of free trade zones (physically enforced by some of the bloodier aspects of the League, particularly its mandate system), combined with limits on production across imperial spheres. This internationalist version of earlier imperial cartels drew simultaneously on wartime cooperation and nineteenth-century imperial practice, now in the name of global collaboration.[28]

Further, the imperial internationalism codified in the peace treaties and in the League's founding documents was based in an already-extant economic and political order produced by Allied military efforts, particularly though not

---

[25] Cited in Jennifer Siegel, 'Planning for an International Financial Order: The Call for Collective Responsibility at the Paris Peace Conference', in Peter Jackson, William Mulligan, Glenda Sluga, eds., *Peacemaking and International Order after the First World War* (Cambridge: Cambridge University Press, 2023), 246–65.
[26] Jamie Martin, 'Raw Materials and International Order', in Peter Jackson, William Mulligan, Glenda Sluga, eds., *Peacemaking and International Order after the First World War* (Cambridge: Cambridge University Press, 2023), 266–86.
[27] Martin, 'Raw Materials', 273; also Mulder, *The Economic Weapon*.
[28] Timothy Mitchell, *Carbon Democracy: Political Power in the Age of Oil*, 2nd ed. (London: Verso, 2023).

exclusively in the Ottoman sphere. Historians' fixation on the thinking of US president Woodrow Wilson, and his disputes with his British and French counterparts, has tended towards allowing the rhetoric of liberal peace-making to obscure this competitive reality of geopolitical outcomes and the basic violence on which the League's global order was based.[29] Even more fundamentally, it also confuses the order of events: for the military, political, and economic basis for League governance rested above all on wartime practices of occupation, resource allocation, and control of populations, all established some time before Wilson declared in Paris that the conference would replace the balance of power with 'a fair and just and honest peace ... in a which the strong and the weak shall fare alike'.[30] By the time an internationalist case was being made for the League's oversight of the Central Powers' former colonies via the new 'mandate' system, the occupations that such words were designed to describe were already fully operational and clearly looking towards the long term. Regimes surrounding refugee encampment, removal, and repatriation, from Eastern Europe to Iraq, were likewise already fleshed-out realities on the ground when they received their rhetorical legitimization via the new League offices. The Allies had also hammered out many of the agreements surrounding the imperial division of crucial resources and raw materials – oil not least among them – during the war itself. In other words, the kind of internationalism that the League promoted was first practically and logistically established in the context of wartime military encounter and *then* described and legitimized as a novel form of promoting international peace, order, and security.

To recap, then, our contention here is this: Making use of nineteenth and early twentieth-century models of imperial accommodation, now joined with practices of inter-Allied wartime cooperation vis-à-vis materials and money, the League of Nations established what international relations scholars might call a global 'order of exclusion': one that would permanently prevent defeated foes (not to mention the Soviet Union) and subaltern League-adhering empires like Italy and Japan from mounting successful challenges to the order dominated by the United States, Britain, and France. Its particular form of ordering had nothing to do with global security for the vast majority of the world's population; it was designed to uphold a long-standing political hierarchy privileging

---

[29] The mismatch between the rhetoric and the reality of peace-making in determining the fate of colonized peoples is analysed in Erez Manela, *The Wilsonian Moment: Self-Determination and the International Origins of Anticolonial Nationalism* (New York: Oxford University Press, 2009).

[30] Harold W. V. Temperley, ed., *A History of the Peace Conference of Paris, Vol. 1* (London: Frowde, 1920), 400.

the interests of the British and French, and now the American, empires above the rest of Europe and permanently sealing colonial territories into a subservient position of resource and labour provisioning – with or without some theoretical form of 'self-determination'.[31]

The United States and the Soviet Union

In this reading, the League was very far from a failure: in fact, as the actual aftermath of the war demonstrated, the League's efforts to build a world order of more or less permanent inequality succeeded brilliantly. Combining the language of liberalism with a commitment to technocracy and 'expertise', the League's practices removed basic questions of resources, labour, migration, and finance from the realm of the political, thereby seeking to protect the imperial powers from the likely objections of a vast majority of the world's population and more broadly to delegitimize popular protest. Further, it built on its members' wartime practice by formally endowing the former Allies with the right to use physical force in 'internationally' governed spaces, strictly regulate global labour and migration, and maintain free trade zones in ways that could ideally be maintained even in the case of some eventual form of independence. (In the event, we might note, these largely did hold – long outlasting the League itself, and surviving any number of forms of sovereignty and independence eventually achieved by the ex-colonial and ex-mandatory territories.)

One of the most important, and most overlooked, aspect of this strategy was its strategic inclusion of the American empire without that nation's formal membership. This new world order depended quite heavily on American participation, not least because of its crucial status as Europe's creditor in the post-war rebuilding efforts. And the same was true in reverse: despite the League's posthumous reputation as an organization of no great power, the United States found its existence and influence to be invaluable as new visions for a specifically American form of economic empire incorporated any number of League practices vis-à-vis labour migration, forcible deportation, and external forms of political/military control in its relations with Mexico and Latin America.[32] Apart from this sharing of influences, the League's 'technical'

---

[31] Adom Getachew, *Worldmaking after Empire: The Rise and Fall of Self-Determination* (Princeton: Princeton University Press, 2019), 37–70.

[32] See Aliki Semertzi, 'Modernist Violence: Juxtaposing the League's Permanent Mandates Commission over the Bondelzwarts Rebellion and the US-Mexico Special Claims Commission over the Mexican Revolution', *Melbourne Journal of International Law* 21/2 (2020), 1–59, and Ronald L. Mize and Alicia C. S. Swords, eds., *Consuming Mexican Labor: From the Bracero Program to NAFTA* (Toronto: University of Toronto Press, 2011).

bodies were the main site for active American participation, particularly the private variety. American private though state-linked organizations (most notably the Rockefeller Foundation and the Carnegie Endowment for International Peace) donated somewhere between $5.5 and $6.5 million to League organizations, with another $10 million coming in to its educational and research initiatives. This set-up guaranteed American influence in interwar internationalism, while shielding the government from the domestic repercussions of official participation.[33] Eventually, this involvement became more formalized. In 1934, the United States formally joined the ILO; in 1940, as the League was threatened by the German triumph, its Economic, Financial, and Trade Department was transferred to Princeton.[34] The US participation in all these bodies served to integrate the scope of American imperial activity into the League's vision for protected zones of economic activity, great power control over raw materials, and limits on migration across the globe.

This truth – and, in fact, the more general realities behind all the League's practices – remained opaque to many liberal observers within the Allied metropoles who were willing to accept many if not all of its claims about commitments to peace, security, and justice and who continued to see the US formal refusal to join as a death blow to internationalist cooperation.[35] It remained opaque even to some degree in the colonies, where hopeful nationalists sometimes saw in the League's messaging (if not in its actual operations) an openness to the possibilities of independence and a more equitable international system. But there was at least one actor on the global stage who understood both the purpose of the League and the American role in it: the emerging Soviet Union. 'That contemptible agency of imperialism,' declared Lenin about the League. 'It has become one of England's diplomatic offices.'[36] Getting to the heart of the League's commitment to the privileges of empire, Lenin also told

---

[33] Ludovic Tournes, *Philanthropic Foundations at the League of Nations: An Americanized League?* trans. Adby Gharibian (London: Routledge, 2022), 24ff.

[34] David Ekbladh, *Plowshares into Swords: Weaponized Knowledge, Liberal Order, and the League of Nations* (Chicago: University of Chicago Press, 2022).

[35] Helen McCarthy, *The British People and the League of Nations: Democracy, Citizenship and Internationalism, 1918–45* (Manchester: Manchester University Press, 2013); Donald Birn, *The League of Nations Union, 1918–1945* (Oxford: Clarendon Press, 1981); Aden Knaap, 'White Internationalism and the League of Nations Movement in Interwar Australia', *Journal of Global History* 19/1 (2024), 77–97.

[36] *Manifesto of the Communist International* (Chicago: Communist Party of America, 1920), 30, 6; quoted in Etienne Henry, 'The Road to Collective Security: Soviet Russia, the League of Nations, and the Emergence of the Ius contra Bellum in the Aftermath of the Russian Revolution (1917–1934)', *Journal of the History of International Law* 355/22 (2020), 355–84. Conservative critics of the League likewise underscored US involvement and interests with the League and its globalizing processes: see Carl Schmitt, *Positionen und Begriffe im Kampf mit Weimar–Genf–Versailles, 1923–1933* (Berlin: Dunker & Humblot, 1988), 100–110.

the British public in 1922 that the League's approach was 'marked by the absence of anything resembling the establishment of the real equality of rights between nations'[37] – a charge clearly demonstrated to be true as the details of the mandate system, among other things, were gradually rolled out. The League's profound hypocrisy on the question of disarmament was likewise highlighted by its rejection of (no less hypocritical) calls by the Soviet Union for total disarmament in the 1920s. Even after the eventual Soviet admission to the League, in 1934, the USSR continued to act as a kind of gadfly pointing out the organization's failures and insincerities. One early historian of the League, speaking of Maxim Litvinov's commentaries in his role as People's Commissar for Foreign Affairs, understood Soviet critiques as among the sharpest observations of the moment: 'Nothing in the annals of the League can compare with them in frankness, in debating power, in the acute analysis of each situation.'[38]

At the same time, the construction of the Soviet state also at times reflected the goals and priorities of the League of which its representatives were officially so critical. Lenin and then Stalin, too, were interested in the creation of novel imperial spaces; in the protection of markets; in state and superstate control over migration and labour; in finding ways to guarantee supplies of raw materials and stabilizing credit; and in configuring the rules of warfare and arms control to favour the spread of revolution and to outlaw an invasion of the Soviet Union. If American forms of influence in Latin America at times resembled mandatory authority, so too did Soviet policy vis-à-vis its own varied subject peoples. Further, the Soviets sometimes sought to create their own forms of internationalism that reflected imperial hierarchies much as the League's did; if the United States understood internationalism as a potentially valuable ally in its construction of a new kind of post-war economic empire, so too did the Soviet Union.[39] The eventual construction of a United Nations with the imprimatur of both the United States and the USSR reflected, perhaps, a clarified understanding on the part of all of the Allies about what this new version of the League was actually intended to do. As Stalin would put it in 1944, what mattered was 'not that there are differences, but that these differences do not transgress the bounds of what the interests of the unity of the three Great Powers allow'.[40] In its revised iteration, there would be no question about whose interests this form of internationalism was built to serve.

---

[37] Henry, 'The Road to Collective Security', 365.
[38] Francis Paul Walters, *A History of the League of Nations* (London: Praeger, 1960), 585.
[39] Terry Martin, *The Affirmative Action Empire: Nations and Nationalism in the Soviet Union, 1923–1939* (Ithaca, NY: Cornell University Press, 2001).
[40] Geoffrey Roberts, 'A League of Their Own', *Journal of Contemporary History* 54/2 (2019), 303–27.

The argument that liberal internationalism, in the shape of an admittedly deeply flawed but at least sometimes well-intentioned, League, unwittingly sowed the seeds of its imperial architects' own destruction allows liberal internationalists to claim a double virtue: good intentions vis-à-vis peace, security, and cooperation in the first instance, and an unintended but ultimately productive move towards decolonization in the second. Neither of these claims holds up under close examination.

First of all, the League's founding had next to nothing to do with pacifist aims or new visions of a genuinely internationalist society. Rather, it drew on a variegated combination of nineteenth-century European forms of collaborative, negotiated imperial domination and the immediate wartime collaborations designed to ensure the conditions necessary for an Allied victory (and manifest in the evidently long-term military occupations of the war's later stages). Both of these precursors assumed the virtue in maintaining the world for empire and ensuring conditions of cooperation vis-à-vis threats of imperial dissolution. In this respect, we might well suggest that the League's primary novelty lay not in some new internationalist imaginary but in its active inclusion of American private capital in its program for global imperial rule – and, perhaps, in its active and explicit centring of economic (rather than military or political) foundations of long-term imperial domination.

The argument that the League accidentally opened the door for decolonization by making public its discussions and creating a new sphere for 'talk' is equally mistaken. In fact, the League sought to delegitimize and disempower its anticolonial opponents by ensuring the ultimate meaninglessness of all forms of discursive protest embedded in its operations, from its practice of conveniently vanishing petitions of protest to its mandatory representatives' punitive use of censorship to its near-total sublimation of local representation in the mandate territories. The League's active disappearance of any kind of verbal protest had the effect of forcing local turns to violence – which, of course, could then be interpreted and presented as precisely the kind of 'disorder' the organization's long-term presence was intended to pre-empt. In other words, the League's active production of discursive venues for public objection that would have no meaningful outcome did two things, both more or less deliberate: it denuded peaceful protest of any political power, and it encouraged the emergence of non-peaceful forms of protest whose evident threat could further and extend League influence in the colonial world, perhaps forever.[41]

---

[41] Jane Cowan, 'Who's Afraid of Violent Language? Honour, Sovereignty and Claims-Making in the League of Nations', *Anthropological Theory* 3/3 (2003), 271–91.

Of course, this project of order and domination was always a work in progress facing both internal dissent and external pressures; and the League's eventual collapse under multipronged attacks on the post-1918 *status quo* spoke, above all, to the ways in which it was intended to defend a very specific – and, as it turned out, fundamentally unstable – vision for a permanent international, geopolitical, and imperial hierarchy. Nevertheless, its survival through the two decades of the interwar period with many of its basic structures intact served as testament to its longevity and (despite roadblocks) its consistency. Whatever the impressions of a disappointed European public, from the perspective of its more directly governed populations – global labourers working under its regulations, migrants seeking its imprimatur for border entry, and corporations looking to its loans and financial guarantees – the League looked much the same before and after the financial crash of 1929, the Japanese invasion of Manchuria in 1931, and even the German occupation of the demilitarized Rhineland in 1936, all later viewed as markers in the collapse of the internationalist project. Its story did not end even with the war: many of the League's fundamental precepts survived in wholly recognizable form in its next incarnation after 1945, and continue to inform and structure the geopolitical hierarchies of the contemporary era. Indeed, the architects of the League might find the modern world, with its hierarchy of nations all too often understood as a kind of natural and even inevitable geopolitical phenomenon, to serve as a reassuring monument to their continued relevance in a supposedly postcolonial world.

1 Ordering People

Control over territory, resources, and wealth – to be reserved for the use and the benefit of the imperial powers, including the United States – could not be accomplished without first establishing control over populations. In the upheavals following the armistice, the chaotic remaking of population politics via forcible and coerced migrations, border changes, nationalizations and denationalizations, the installation of global labour controls, and the creation of new categories of refugeehood and statelessness all appeared to the League's leadership as both hazard and opportunity as they began to set the stage for a new global order. Though these missions have often been regarded as secondary to the League's security and economic concerns, or set aside as 'technical' operations that could be assessed separately from its more central operations, we begin here for good reason: because this ostensibly scientific, humanitarian, and bureaucratic work actually constituted the bedrock on which the League's political and economic controls would be built.

First among the League's post-war missions was the determination and enforcement of new borders in Central and Eastern Europe and across the old Ottoman territories of what was now being called the Middle East. For all the talk about 'self-determination' and the rights of small nations, the new borders in Eastern Europe, the Balkans, and the Middle East were drawn up mainly with reference to economic and strategic interests of the major powers; the negotiations over them featured a near-total disregard of the interests or preferences of populations on the ground, despite considerable efforts by local actors vis-à-vis questions like Czechoslovakia or an expanded vision of Greece. The settlements sought, in broad strokes, to settle inter-imperial disputes over the boundaries between British and French power and to establish the League as the final arbiter of any post-war map. To this end, it proved convenient that so many of the new state borders produced newly nationalized majorities but also newly emergent 'minorities', long-standing and well-established but now suddenly politically vulnerable communities. Their existence had the undoubted capacity to undermine any number of post-war national projects and threaten the continent's stability; but their evident fragility and their need for some kind of external guarantee of security could also give the League an indisputable raison d'être and serve as a venue for post-war Allied intervention in the affairs of theoretically sovereign states. Such ostensibly bureaucratic mechanisms of 'protection', then, were not mere window dressing; they actively and deliberately formulated the conditions for the Allies to pursue a top-down material and geographical ordering of some of the messiest territorial dispositions of the post-war era.

The physical dislocation of populations likewise represented both problem and solution for the Allies and their League. Wartime and post-war expulsions, particularly the mass flight of Anatolian Christians into Greece as Mustafa Kemal's nationalist armies advanced on Smyrna, suggested to the League the possibility of serving as an institutionalized arbiter of a general 'unmixing of populations', as the British diplomat Lord Curzon had so memorably put it.[42] The League's role in the brutal compulsory population exchange between Greece and Turkey, formalized in the war's final treaty in 1923, made it into a new kind of entity: one that could make or break new states, and that had the power to set the bar of entrance for nationality and citizenship. Here, again, these supposedly benevolent interventions made possible the creation of Allied-ordered states and citizen bodies – not to mention channels of money,

---

[42] There is debate about the origins of this phrase, uttered by both Curzon and Fridtjof Nansen, it may have been first proposed by Philip Noel-Baker, whose early proposals for a 'real unmixing of Balkan populations' served as a basis for conversation at Lausanne. See Matthew Frank, *Making Minorities History: Population Transfer in Twentieth-Century Europe* (Oxford: Oxford University Press, 2017), chapter 2.

investment, and development – that belied the League's presentation of its actions as humanitarian and 'technical' rather than political, economic, or military.

Mass dislocation offered other kinds of opportunities as well. For those not to be renationalized by forcible transfer, the League created novel documentary categories controlled by its member states: most notably the so-called Nansen Passport, an early experiment in remaking refugees into guest workers whose labour could serve as an asset to willing host countries. For the next decade, the League sought to place refugees in low-wage employment outside Europe – particularly in Latin America, where such provision of workers could tie together the interests of the European empires and a United States increasingly invested, both economically and politically, in its southern neighbours. This kind of labour migration could also help support an order to which the League was very deeply committed indeed: a global hierarchy of wages and working conditions. The League repeatedly and publicly declared its dedication to the protection of workers in the metropoles while ensuring the legalized continuation of sub-par conditions and remuneration, including internationally authorized forced labour, in the colonies. In its external setting of the conditions for highly inequitable forms of international labour distribution and remuneration, the League was establishing a crucial mode of global economic control that might be able to survive any number of shifts in the political winds.

And finally, the League found still another way of controlling populations: through direct rule. Its 'international administration' of the Free City of Danzig and the mandatory territory of the Saar gave the League a new avenue for its pursuit of political power. This direct assertion of political power over some of Europe's most contested land, over the protests of their populations, provided venues for thinking through the practicalities of a technocratic internationalist rule: one that would claim a progressive modern politics while actively suppressing claims to democratic representation in the actual territories it controlled. Technical capacity, developmentalist expertise, and humanitarian intervention did not constitute some secondary level of League practice to be judged in isolation. To the contrary, these were the basic tools that laid the groundwork for the League's political and economic ordering of the globe to benefit its primary members.

The Making of Borders

Quite early on in its tenure, the League's Allied constituencies coalesced around two apparently irreconcilable ideas about borders. On the one hand, they hoped for the eventual re-emergence of a global system of open trade and passport-free travel, a return to the economic conditions of nineteenth-century imperial liberalism. On the other, they were also increasingly committed to the idea that visible and enforceable borders were a crucial element of the geopolitical order their League was building – an idea that came out of an already-extant hope in imperial circles, especially the British variety, that rising nationalisms across the empire and the globe could be turned to imperial advantage.

The rising fortunes of racialist thought gave a decisive boost to the second impulse. The early 1920s saw the former Allied powers, for the first time in their histories, doubling down on broad and punitive immigration restrictions as a protective measure, understood in both ethnic and economic terms. 'It is preached that the highest human type is the Nordic type, the fair-haired and blue-eyed people of North Europe,' one newspaper in Jamaica reported on this new development, 'and the aim of those in America who have been captivated by this doctrine is to keep America for the Nordic type.'[43] Such racial interpretations of these new policies were not mistaken. One of the League's main architects, the South African politician and writer Jan Smuts, rooted his original vision in the concept of white supremacy and segregation – a vision shared across the Allied political landscape and inclusive of American thinkers like Woodrow Wilson. As Smuts put it in 1930, 'The mixing up of two such alien elements as white and black leads to unhappy social results – racial miscegenation, moral deterioration of both, racial antipathy and clashes, and to many other forms of social evil'[44] – an assessment that tracked closely with Wilson's own positions vis-à-vis race and segregation, not to mention long-standing racial assumptions of British and French imperial thought.[45]

Further bolstering the idea of defined, defensible borders were old lines of thought about how nationhood and nationalism could represent valuable new venues for imperial clientelism. From the nineteenth century forward, for instance, the emergence of Greek national claims against the Ottoman Empire came to be seen as a path to British influence over a weak and peripheral state. The 'protection' of Maronite Christians in Mount Lebanon similarly appeared

---

[43] Cited in Lara Putnam, 'Unspoken Exclusions: Race, Nation, and Empire in the Immigration Restrictions of the 1920s in North America and the Greater Caribbean', in Leon Fink, ed., *Workers across the Americas: The Transnational Turn in Labor History* (Oxford: Oxford University Press, 2011), 267–94.

[44] Jan Smuts, *Africa and Some World Problems* (Oxford: Clarendon Press, 1930), 93; see also Jacob Kripp, 'The Creative Advance Must Be Defended: Miscegenation, Metaphysics, and Race War in Jan Smuts's Vision of the League of Nations', *American Political Science Review* 116/3 (2022), 940–53.

[45] Saul Dubow, 'Smuts, the United Nations and the Rhetoric of Race and Rights', *Journal of Contemporary History* 43 (2008), 45–74; Jeanne Morefield, *Empires without Imperialism: Anglo-American Decline and the Politics of Deflection* (New York: Oxford University Press, 2014); and Mark Mazower, *No Enchanted Palace*.

to open up new possibilities for French commercial, military, and political presence in greater Syria. Sometimes, active engagement with nationalisms became an explicit strategy for turning forms of anti-colonial protest into submerged aspects of imperial rule. The admission of the possibility of Home Rule for Ireland, for instance, remade an Irish national identity formed in active opposition to the British Empire into an acknowledged constituent part of imperial governance, taming its anti-imperialism and transforming it into an updated form of British oversight. In still another instance, Jewish nationalism appeared as a potentially useful ally for the British empire in the Middle East in the form of a politically indebted European settler movement in Palestine. The increased attention the United States brought during and after the war to the question of the rights of 'small nations' further reinforced this sense of the potential utility of nationalism for updated forms of empire. The advantages of a world of racialized nation-states for the Allied empires, then, quickly came to seem incontrovertible, even as the fantasy of reconstructing the nineteenth century's easy-access order also retained its allure. The eventual compromise between these two visions would be simple: open borders for goods, closed borders for people.

The peacemakers at Paris (and then at St. Germain, Trianon, Sèvres, and Lausanne) had been charged as a first task with the determination of borders in central and eastern Europe and the old Ottoman Empire as the demolition of the old land empires got underway. Their new demarcations, recommended by appointed territorial commissions made up of 'experts' like geographers and economists, now considered how to construct new nation-states with primary reference to raw materials and networks of trade. Hungary's need for imported coal, for instance, formed a backdrop for its ceding of Slovakia to Czechoslovakia, a coal exporter.[46] The drawing of the border between Syria and Iraq followed intensive negotiations between the British and the French about the ownership of Iraq's oil, with a final settlement awarding the territory of Mosul to British Iraq on the condition that France would receive a permanent 25 per cent share of Iraqi oil and the additional right to buy a quarter of the oil shipped through French-controlled territory.[47] In Transylvania, the assignment of the region to Romania was carefully designed not to disrupt the prosperity of Magyar, Jewish, and German elites and businesses there; in 1919 the French, backed by a military force stationed there, blocked the new Romanian

---

[46] Aliaksandr Piahanau, '"Each Wagon of Coal Should Be Paid for with Territorial Concessions": Hungary, Czechoslovakia, and the Coal Shortage in 1918–21', *Diplomacy and Statecraft* 34/1 (2023), 86–116.

[47] Luigi Scazzieri, 'Britain, France, and Mesopotamian Oil, 1916–1920', *Diplomacy & Statecraft* 26/1 (2015), 25–45.

government's effort to nationalize foreign-owned companies. 'There are two bastions that the bayonet of the Romanian peasant has not yet been able to conquer: industry and commerce,' one Romanian observer complained. 'More than ever before they are in the hands of our fellow citizens of another nationality.'[48] In other words, despite Keynes' famous post-war claims that the new borders had wilfully destroyed the economies of Eastern Europe, in fact the territorial commissions mostly put into place systems that reinforced older central and eastern European trade patterns and ensured continued access for foreign interests.[49] The simultaneous carving up of the Middle East into national 'mandate' states likewise followed on resource-related rationales, particularly those related to oil.[50]

Even as the post-war commissions worked to maintain the openness of foreign trade and mechanisms of foreign ownership, though, the League was committing to strict controls over the movement of workers – making use of concepts of nationalism to defend borders put in place for quite other reasons. 'Recruiting of bodies of workers ... should not be permitted,' the ILO declared in one of its earliest recommendations, 'except by mutual agreement between the countries interested and after consultation with employers and workers in each country in the industries concerned.'[51] It was clear to all concerned that control over the roiling population politics of the newly divided territories of eastern Europe, the Balkans, and the Arab Eastern Mediterranean was key to accomplishing the Allied goal of an ordered map of ethnically defined nation-states whose resources were broadly under the control of, or at least permanently accessible to, the imperial powers.

The Question of Minorities

Such international control over both goods and people required a new set of practical tools, legal and institutional frameworks, and political justifications. The narrative of 'minority protection' played a crucial role in the construction

---

[48] Máté Rigó, 'The Long First World War and the Survival of Business Elites in East-Central Europe: Transylvania's Industrial Boom and the Enrichment of Economic Elites', *European Review of History: Revue Européene d'Histoire* 24/2 (2017), 250–272.

[49] John Maynard Keynes, *Economic Consequents of the Peace* (London: Harcourt, 1919), versus Nikolaus Wold, Max-Stephan Schulze, and Hans-Christian Heinemeyer, 'On the Economic Consequences of the Peace: Trade and Borders After Versailles', *Journal of Economic History* 71/4 (2011), 915–49.

[50] Leonard Smith, 'Drawing Borders in the Middle East after the Great War: Political Geography and "Subject Peoples"', *First World War Studies* 7/1 (2015), 5–21.

[51] ILO Unemployment Recommendation, 1919, cited in Leila Kawar, 'Assembling an International Social Protection for the Migrant: Juridical Categorization in ILO Migration Standards, 1919–1939', *Global Social Policy* 22/2 (2022), 244–62.

and legitimization of procedural methods for retaining Allied oversight over populations within theoretically sovereign states.

From its inception, the League was assigned responsibility for the protection of communities newly designated as 'minorities' in post-war states whose territorial bounds had been redefined. Poland, Yugoslavia, Czechoslovakia, Albania, Lithuania, Estonia, Iraq, and Latvia all signed treaties guaranteeing minority protections with the Allied powers; Austria, Bulgaria, Hungary, and Turkey were subject to similar minority protections regimes enshrined in the broader treaties of Saint-Germain, Neuilly, Trianon, and Sèvres. These guaranteed minorities' rights to acquire citizenship; to equal treatment including access to public office; to use minority languages and establish and maintain cultural institutions; and to access a proportional share of public money for purposes like education.

It was immediately evident to observers from across the political spectrum that in actuality this minority protection regime would do next to nothing to advance the welfare of Hungarians in Romania or Germans in Czechoslovakia. The League's Minorities Section, housed in the Secretariat, was charged with receiving petitions that alleged infractions of the treaties with respect to minorities – the only direct route to the League for any minority complaints. If the section determined that the petition was 'receivable' – a standard rarely met[52] – it was passed on to the relevant state, which could offer a rebuttal. Then, a committee made up of League Council members would discuss the case; if it had merit, the League Council would attempt to reach a consensus with a representative of the offending state. This system, such as it was, was clearly designed to ensure that vanishingly few cases would reach the Council, and even fewer would see any kind of redress.

What, then, was the real purpose of the Minorities Section and the broader promotion of League responsibility for minority rights? In the first instance, it represented a reinvention of nineteenth-century schemes that had premised European commercial, political, and military intervention in the old Ottoman realms on the fiction of 'protecting' certain Christian communities there, particularly Armenians. The Treaty of Berlin, signed in 1878, tied the rights of foreign corporations in the Ottoman state to 'religious liberty' for minorities and appointed the Great Powers 'superintendents' of their efforts. The independence of Serbia, Montenegro, and Romania were also premised on parallel guarantees for foreign 'traders' and local 'freedom of all forms of worship'. Now, the minority treaties did the same thing: 'The Great Powers ... lay down conditions on which they transfer the territories to such State,' the treaty for Poland ran. 'In

---

[52] Cowan, 'Who's Afraid of Violent Language'?

the future no distinction shall be made between citizens in consequence of difference of race, religion, or language ... In addition to this we have provision by which Poland undertakes not to make any discrimination against the commerce of any of the Allied and Associated Powers.'[53] In other words, the idea that the rights of certain religious communities could serve as an entrée for privileged forms of European commercial presence was an old imperial practice, even if the neologism of minority gave it some new and modern valences.[54]

Second, the Minorities Section provided the League with a venue for outlining a hierarchy of state sovereignty: there were some states whose minorities needed no protections, and others who – ostensibly because of their civilizational stage – had to be firmly bound by such guarantees. This differentiation aroused fury in the targeted states, whose representatives fully understood the ramifications of this kind of monitoring. As the Romanian representative to the League protested, the minorities treaties established 'two categories of countries – countries of the first class, which, in spite of having small groups of minorities, were placed under no obligations; and countries of the second class, which had been obliged to assume extremely onerous obligations.'[55] (This distinction mirrored practices in the economic sphere, as many of the same countries were finding themselves subject to punishing regimes of austerity as a condition of currency-stabilizing loans.) The minorities system served to reinforce a global order in which some nations would have to accept substantial external interventions as a price of their territory. As the Lithuanian-born jurist Jacob Robinson put it, 'In the Versailles peace system, the minorities provisions constituted a corollary and corrective to the principle of national self-determination.'[56]

Finally, as historian Carolyn Biltoft points out, the section explicitly conceived of the petitions it received as 'informational' rather than actionable; they provided 'a source of intelligence, observation, and intervention into territories and became a route for protecting certain geopolitical interests, a kind of proxy imperial command center'.[57] In other words, the Minorities Section's collection of petitions it never intended to consider seriously made it into an information-gathering agency for the Allied powers interested in maintaining access to

---

[53] Harold Temperley, *A History of the Peace Conference of Paris*, Vol. 5 (London: Frowde, 1924), 143–44.
[54] For a broader presentation of this argument, see Robson, 'Capitulations Redux'.
[55] League of Nations Council, *Protection of Linguistic, Racial or Religious Minorities* (Geneva: League of Nations, 1929), 45.
[56] Jacob Robinson, Oscar Karbach, Max M. Laserson, et al., *Were the Minorities Treaties a Failure?* (New York: Institute of Jewish Affairs, 1943), 41.
[57] Carolyn Biltoft, 'The Meek Shall Not Inherit the Earth: National Minorities and National Economies at the League of Nations', in Christoph Kreutzmuller, Michael Wildt, and Moshe Zimmermann, eds., *National Economies: Volks-Wirtschaft, Racism and Economy in Europe between the Wars (1918–1939/45)* (Newcastle: Cambridge Scholars, 2015), 138–54.

information about affected states' conditions and resources while limiting Russian, Turkish, and German access to the same. The data it gathered could be put to any number of purposes by the 'technical' bodies of the League, concerned with matters of investment, development, and resources.

Refugees and 'Humanitarianism'

In this moment of rising nationalisms and hardening borders, then, the issue of mass displacement loomed large at the League, where contradictory interests jostled around the question of settling the war's refugees. In the first instance, most of the displaced whom the League understood as an international problem were 'White Russians', people driven from Bolshevik territory through some association with tsarist interests and/or participation in the White Army. Russian refugees of this sort were not just a site of upheaval and uncertainty for the emerging post-war nation-states of central and eastern Europe; they also stood as a symbol of the political struggle between an emergent Soviet Bolshevism and the liberal-imperial political order of Western Europe and North America. Given these ideological stakes, we should perhaps be unsurprised that the first efforts to do something about the hundreds of thousands of refugees scattered around eastern and central Europe approached the issue as a problem of labour. In 1921 a collection of relief organizations, including the Red Cross and Save the Children as well as some Russian agencies, approached the newly constituted International Labour Organization with a plan to solve the issue of displacement by putting refugees back to work (see Figure 4). The League agreed that mass displacement was clearly correlated with issues of post-war labour distribution and that those dislocated by Bolshevism should be rehabilitated primarily through the liberal internationalist provision of gainful employment.

Such a task offered new legitimacy to the League, which presented itself as a novel agency with an unchallenged and unparalleled capacity to settle such post-war issues. The League, Red Cross president Gustave Ador declared happily, was 'the only supranational political authority capable of solving a problem which was beyond the power of exclusively humanitarian organizations'.[58] In September of 1921, a Norwegian former polar explorer turned diplomat named Fridjtof Nansen accepted a new position at the League of Nations: High Commissioner for Russian Refugees. His task was not just to resettle refugees who were increasingly viewed as incendiary elements in the already unstable post-war European landscape but to mould them into object lessons in anti-Bolshevism, a task being taken up in more general terms by the ILO. As the American commentator James Shotwell put it,

---

[58] Cited in Atle Grahl-Madsen, 'The League of Nations and the Refugees', in *The League of Nations in Retrospect* (Berlin: De Gruyter, 2010), 358–68.

Figure 4 In March 1920, the Red Cross reported that 'About thirty children who got lost from their parents during the rush of refugees to leave the doomed city of Novorossisk, in South Russia found themselves well taken care of. They were all gathered together and taken to the Crimea by the American Red Cross on the relief ship Sangammon. This picture shows some of the children in charge of Lieut. L.M.

Foster, of Chicago. Many of the children were restored to their parents after reaching the Crimea, while those whose parents could not be located were taken to the Red Cross colony on the island of Proti where they are being well cared for.'

Library of Congress, American National Red Cross photograph collection.

'The Allied Governments had to offer to labor some definite and formal recognition at the very opening of the Conference ... to prove to the workers of the world that the principles of social justice might be established under the capitalist system.'[59]

Selling the idea of allowing refugees in as workers, though, proved difficult. The idea that sovereign states might have the right to bar entry to foreigners was not well established prior to this period; indeed, as late as 1914 there was no legal consensus in Europe around this question.[60] But the early 1920s became a moment of near-total border closure in Britain, much of Western Europe, the Soviet Union, and – arguably with greatest effect – the United States, following

---

[59] James T. Shotwell, 'The International Labor Organization as an Alternative to Violent Revolution', *ANNALS of the American Political Science Association* 166/1 (1933), 18–25.

[60] John Torpey, 'Coming and Going: On the State Monopolization of the Legitimate "Means of Movement"', *Sociological Theory* 16/3 (1998), 239–59.

decades in which some 97 per cent of immigrants entering the United States through Ellis Island were admitted without objection. In the United Kingdom, efforts to keep Eastern European Jews out had begun to gather momentum with the Aliens Act of 1905 and were now solidifying into more general restrictions. In the United States, the Secretary of State declared that a new circumspection was in order: 'Our restriction on immigration should be so rigid that it would be impossible for most of these people to enter the United States.'[61] In the Soviet Union, the denationalization of 'White Russian' refugees went hand-in-hand with the closure of its (still emerging) borders, a scheme intended more to prevent emigration than immigration but that also had the effect of disallowing refugee return. Even in Latin America, long considered a space for possible migration and a safety valve for 'surplus' populations, governments were beginning to express doubts about the acceptance of large numbers of migrants and construct new barriers to entry.

It was in this context, then, that Nansen constructed a different plan: not one of integration or citizenship but of temporary residence premised mainly on employment. The so-called Nansen Passport was a new type of document, emerging at more or less the same time as the more general and increasingly standardized passport regime. Sixteen signatory governments agreed to issue identification documents to refugees within their borders, who would henceforth generally have permission (which could, however, be denied without explanation) to move through these countries in search of work. The participating states were not bound by this agreement, which in any case offered nothing in the way of access to citizenship. Initially, these were designed solely for *personnes d'origine russe* and were valid for a single year at a time. If the bearer acquired another nationality, the Nansen Passport would be rendered void. In time this system was expanded, though not to all displaced people; Armenian refugees became eligible for the passport in 1924, and a smaller number of Assyrians and related Christian 'minorities', mainly from eastern Anatolia, in 1928. There were also some extensions of its implications, with the addition of a right to a return visa in 1926 and the provision of certain refugee services via the League (certification of identity, offering character testimony, and recommending refugees to employers and other institutions) in 1928. The number of participating nations dropped with each addition; fifty-four states recognized the passport for Russians, but only thirty-eight for Armenians, and just thirteen for Assyrians and Chaldeans.[62]

---

[61] *New York Times*, 20 April 1920; cited in Benjamin Alexander, 'Armenian and American: The Changing Face of Ethnic Identity and Diasporic Nationalism, 1915–1955' (PhD dissertation, City University of New York, 2005), 111.

[62] John Torpey, *The Invention of the Passport: Surveillance, Citizenship and the State* (Cambridge: Cambridge University Press, 2009), 128–29.

What should we make of this system? The scholarly consensus on the Nansen passport has paralleled the conversation around the League more generally, with an assessment that it represented an effortful, meaningful, and good-faith first effort to resolve the contradictions of a global system of nation-states that was producing unprecedented numbers of stateless people. Indeed, it is often regarded as the first step towards formalized international legal protections for the displaced; as historian Claudena Skran wrote long ago, 'The beginning of international refugee law can properly be dated to the creation of the Nansen passport system.'[63] In another much-quoted phrase, Michael Marrus judged it to be a crucial and substantive legal innovation: 'For the first time it permitted determination of the juridical status of stateless persons through a specific international agreement ... [and] allowed an international agency, the High Commission, to act for those whom their countries of origin had rejected.'[64] For many decades, then, it was received as a humanitarian success that both assisted displaced people in the moment and pointed the way to later advances in refugee law and refugee rights.

To consider the validity of this interpretation, we should think about the specifics of how the Nansen Passport worked. First of all, refugees had to pay to apply for it; the charge was five gold francs. Each issuing state had its own format and its own set of information; the only feature that unified these various national iterations was the inclusion of the 'Nansen stamp', without which the documents would be declared useless.[65] The passports quickly became a useful source of information about the direction, numbers, and conditions of Russian refugees in various places – data that was used to try to move refugees into states nearer to the Soviet Union, particularly Poland and Finland.[66] The requirement that they had to be renewed every year allowed for heightened surveillance of refugee holders of these documents, and re-applications were often denied. The acquisition of this passport in itself guaranteed nothing to the bearer, not even the right not to be deported; it was an informal gesture of accession that could be withdrawn or not recognized at will. Still, a great number of people wanted one: the issuing countries produced some four hundred and fifty thousand Nansen passports over the course of the program's life.

There were some ironies embedded in the outcomes of the Nansen passport system. In the first instance, the League itself, despite its developing commitment

---

[63] Claudena Skran, *Refugees in Interwar Europe: The Emergence of a Regime* (Oxford: Clarendon Press, 1995), 105.
[64] Michael Marrus, *The Unwanted: European Refugees from the First World War Through the Cold War* (Oxford: Oxford University Press, 1985), 95.
[65] Kacey Bengal, 'Understanding the Nansen Passport: A System of Manipulation', *Indiana Journal of Global Legal Studies* 29/1 (2022), 217–32.
[66] Bengal, 'Understanding the Nansen Passport'.

Figure 5 Nansen Passport renewal stamp featuring head of Fridtjof Nansen, 1930. Public domain.

to the concept of borders and the political framework of the sovereign nation-state, was also experimenting with ideas of return to the nineteenth-century system of open borders that had been such a crucial element of pre-war liberal internationalism. It held two international meetings on the topic of cross-border mobility, in 1920 and 1926, both of which pressed member states to abandon efforts at border control and get rid of the emerging international passport regime altogether.[67] (A resolution from the 1920 conference acknowledged that contemporary conditions made impossible 'the total abolition of restrictions and that complete return to pre-war conditions which the Conference hopes, nevertheless, to see gradually re-established in the near future.'[68]) In some respects, it is possible to imagine that when the Nansen Passport was conceived its architects were looking hopefully towards a future when statelessness would once again be an essentially meaningless category, as passports were abolished and an older freedom of movement was reinstated (see Figure 5).

In practice, though, the promulgation of the Nansen Passport helped substantially to fortify theories and practices of border control: it assumed that national

---

[67] Peter Becker, 'Remaking Mobility: International Conferences and the Emergence of the Modern Passport System', in Peter Becker and Natasha Wheatley, eds., *Remaking Central Europe: The League of Nations and the Former Habsburg Lands*, (Oxford: Oxford University Press, 2020), 193–212.

[68] League of Nations, *Conference on Passports, Customs Formalities, and Through Tickets* (Geneva: League of Nations, 1920), 1.

sovereignty necessarily carried with it the right to restrict migrant entry, and explicitly made refugees dependent on the goodwill and/or the immediate labour needs of individual states for entrance, residence, and return. It was an outcome reinforced by the 1926 League conference on passports. 'Braving unpopularity, but conscious of the responsibilities of the Governments represented,' the conference's president summed up, 'had decided that the time was not yet ripe for the total abolition of passports throughout the world ... The travellers' passport would continue – at any rate for the present – to be the conventional inter-State permit' – now regularized, standardized, and coordinated among states. Refugee documentation would be part of this recalibration; as the conference reported, 'the Technical Sub-Committee had already discussed the question as to how far this subject was connected with the problem of Armenian and Russian refugees ... the question of method was to be left to the Committee of Experts.'[69] Far from being a temporary expedient, the Nansen Passport had proven to be an augur: of an evermore bounded and bordered future, to be sure, but also of a world in which the mechanics, operation, and legitimization of border controls would be actively recategorized as 'technical' rather than political questions, removed from the hurly-burly of national electoral politics into the rarefied atmosphere of international expertise.

Expulsions and Resettlements

The League's imperative to create and preserve national order seemed, in some instances, to require the active removal and resettlement of whole populations to ensure regional 'security' and provide permanent avenues for internationalist intervention. These schemes, falling somewhere between its minority protection and refugee aid regimes, sought to provide the great powers with a political landscape clearly organized around nationality, in which Western political oversight and commercial involvement would have clear and legitimized national channels. It was a goal that, in their view, fully justified the suffering such schemes inevitably caused.

The practice of internationalist removal – what British Foreign Secretary George Curzon called the 'unmixing of peoples'[70] – had precursors, of course: most notably, the many and violent expulsions and resettlements that took place between the Balkans, the Caucasus, and Ottoman Anatolia in the second half of the nineteenth century, including proposals for population swaps. In the more immediate past, iterations of this idea had been floated at the Paris talks: by

---

[69] League of Nations, *Passport Conference Held at Geneva from May 12th to 18th, 1926* (Geneva: League of Nations, 1926), 50.
[70] The genesis of this phrase is discussed in Christopher Smith, ed., *Sovereignty: A Global Perspective*, (Oxford: Oxford University Press, 2023), chapter 4.

Eduard Benes, for instance, who proposed exchanging Magyars and Slovaks between Hungary and Slovakia. In 1919, the first international test of such plans came with the scheme, constructed mainly by Greek prime minister Eleutherios Venizelos, for a theoretically voluntary 'exchange' between Greece and Bulgaria – a scheme to which the Allies acceded fairly easily. It was a short step to the next exchange, which this time would be compulsory.

The Greek–Turkish war of the early 1920s, which resulted in Mustafa Kemal's (later Ataturk) defeat of the Greek armies, the end of the 'Megáli Idéa' of a greater Greece extending into Anatolia, and the establishment and recognition of an independent Republic of Turkey, had caused the dislocation of hundreds of thousands of Anatolian Christians fleeing the Turkish nationalist militias. Most of them had left for Greece and more were coming all the time, especially after the terrible fire in 1922 that destroyed Smyrna, long the centre of Orthodox life in Anatolia. In the aftermath of the conflict, Greek prime minister Eleftherios Venizelos and the League's own Fridtjof Nansen agreed with Mustafa Kemal on the outlines of a scheme to evict Orthodox Christians from Anatolia and Muslims from Greece once and for all. In 1923, at Lausanne, the Allied powers signed the final treaty of the First World War, which provided for a 'compulsory exchange' of Turkey's Christians and Greece's Muslims: 'These persons shall not return to live in Turkey or Greece respectively without the authorisation of the Turkish Government or of the Greek Government respectively (see Figure 6).'[71] Not incidentally, the treaty also assigned the oil-rich territory of Mosul to British-controlled Iraq, apportioned the Ottoman debt among the empire's successor states, and limited the use of tariffs for some years, all in the continuing tradition of using population politics as a venue for the general allocation of territory and resources.

There were plenty of objections to the terms of Lausanne, which even at the time appeared to many observers as indefensibly brutal and probably illegal under the rules of international diplomacy. The Greek lawyer C.G. Tenekides, Venizelos' legal adviser at the Lausanne talks and author of an early French-language study of the exchange, called it a 'regrettable regression in the evolution of human rights'.[72] Even Curzon himself declared it 'a thoroughly bad and vicious solution, for which the world would pay a heavy penalty for a hundred years to come', and publicly regretted his own involvement: 'he detested having anything to do with it.'[73] And indeed, the consequences were dire. The treaty

---

[71] Treaty of Lausanne, Article 1. Treaty of Peace with Turkey, signed at Lausanne on July 24, 1923, available at: https://treaties.fcdo.gov.uk/data/Library2/pdf/TS0016.1923.pdf.

[72] C. Georges Tenekides, 'Le statut des minorités et l'échange obligatoire des populations gréco-turques', *Revue générale de droit international public* 31/1–2 (1924), 76.

[73] Conference on Near Eastern Affairs, *Records of Proceedings and Draft Terms of Peace*, Vol. 1 (London: HMSO, 1923), 212.

Figure 6 'Refugees in front of the ruins of the temple of Thesus [Theseus]', Anatolian refugees photographed by Red Cross aid workers, Athens, 1922. Library of Congress, American National Red Cross photograph collection.

triggered the expulsion of the remaining Christians in Anatolia nearly without exception; tens of thousands of them died on their way to their new 'homeland'. Greek Muslims, expelled mainly from Macedonia and Thrace, likewise suffered massive casualties on the journey and found themselves destitute upon arrival. As historian Eric Weitz has memorably put it, 'population exchange' and 'unmixing' were 'pallid phrases [that] masked the sheer misery and desperation of the Muslims and Christians who were being forced out of their ancestral homes'. He added, 'For each group, the integration into the Greek of Turkish national state and society was a wrenching experience that continued over generations, traces of which can still be found today.'[74]

This phenomenally violent scheme, which many scholars now understand as an ethnic cleansing, received the enthusiastic imprimatur of Nansen's refugee office and the League more generally. For Nansen and for the League Secretariat, the mechanics of the exchange offered an unparalleled opportunity to demonstrate the utility of internationalism to both the empires and their emerging client states. The goal, as Nansen himself made explicit in arguing for the exchange, was to render both Greece and Turkey safe spaces for capital investment; ethnic order was 'of real importance to the peace and economic stability of the Near East',[75] and the exchange represented 'the quickest and most efficacious way of dealing with the grave economic results which must result from the great movement of populations which has already occurred'.[76] He connected these two ideas by constructing a scheme under which the Bank of England would issue bonds backing a large loan to the Greek government for the purpose of resettling Anatolian refugees on Macedonian farmland (mostly expropriated from its former Muslim owners and inhabitants).[77] The ethnic homogenization of these spaces was thus turned into a project both of state construction and Western investment – including American financiers, who were, as one historian notes, 'perfectly willing to use [the League] as a way of controlling their assets in foreign states'.[78] The US State Department actively participated in the committee on loan conditions and sent a representative to the League of Nations Council to approve its recommendations, and the former American ambassador (and Wilsonian delegation member) Henry Morgenthau was tapped to head up the Greek Refugee Settlement Commission administering the money.[79]

The League's involvement in population politics in the Balkans, then, served a number of goals at once: producing viable, stable, nationally homogenous Allied client states engaged in processes of economic modernization, especially along the *cordon sanitaire* that separated Europe from the Soviets; creating a new global economy in which Western (including American) money operated

---

[74] Eric Weitz, 'From the Vienna to the Paris System: International Politics and the Entangled Histories of Human Rights, Forced Deportations, and Civilizing Missions', *American Historical Review* 113/5 (2009), 1313–43; also Bruce Clark, *Twice a Stranger: The Mass Expulsions that Forged Greece and Turkey* (Cambridge, MA: Harvard University Press, 2009).

[75] Umut Özsu, 'Fabricating Fidelity: Nation-Building, International Law, and the Greek–Turkish Population Exchange', *Leiden Journal of International Law* 24/4 (2011), 823–47.

[76] Great Britain Parliamentary Papers, *Turkey No. 1 (1923) Lausanne Conference on Near Eastern Affairs, 1922–1923* (London: HMSO, 1923), 117.

[77] Stephen Ladas, *The Exchange of Minorities: Bulgaria, Greece and Turkey* (New York: Macmillan, 1932), 720; Frank, *Making Minorities History,* 92.

[78] Biltoft, 'The Meek Shall Not', 148.

[79] Tournes, *Philanthropic Foundations at the League of Nations,* 27.

to expand both production and markets across widely dispersed territory, with or without a context of active political control; and creating venues for an Allied institutional presence on the ground in the form of aid provision and loan monitoring. The fact that the work being undertaken was in service of what future generations would think of as a brutal ethnic cleansing – one with tens of thousands of casualties – made little impact on the official narrative, which for many decades touted the exchange and the League's part in it as a success story for nationalism and internationalism alike.

The Technicalities of Labour: Refugees and Workers at the ILO

In 1925 Nansen managed to reassign most of the work of his High Commission for Refugees to the ILO, on the basis of its technical and 'scientific' expertise in distributing and protecting workers around the globe. From this point onward, the League's refugee services revolved almost entirely around the provision of employment. The ILO's refugee services and the remaining part of the Nansen High Commission for Refugees collectively served as a kind of clearinghouse for matching refugees with jobs (mainly menial labour in agricultural and industrial concerns); facilitating refugee employment via the provision of medical and security screenings; legal assistance with visas and travel documents; and loaning refugees money (usually involving interest) for transport and settlement costs. This employment was, in the main, to be located as far from Western Europe as possible. 'As a result of the uneasiness awakened by the preliminary symptoms of an economic crisis in France,' the ILO's Governing Council reported in 1928, 'it began to be thought that difficult as it was to transport the refugees to distant countries, it would be better to attempt to settle large numbers of refugees as permanent colonists, particularly in South America.'[80]

The League was especially interested in Latin America as a destination for refugee workers, perhaps partly because such schemes correlated with a variety of American plans for foreign-funded development there. Indeed, it was common for North American companies to approach the League in search of cheap workers. The Canadian-owned Sao Paolo Tramway, Light and Power Company, in Brazil, sought 3,000 unskilled workers for the construction of a new power plant in 1925. In Paraguay, the American-owned International Products Company told the commission that 'the Company was very interested in colonisation'.[81] The League itself sometimes compared this sort of refugee migration to Latin America to the

---

[80] International Labour Organization, *Minutes of the 38: Session of the GB of the ILO* (Geneva: League of Nations, 1928), 173.
[81] 'Report on the Work for the Refugees', League of Nations *Official Journal*, special supplement 58 (1925), 135.

settlement of the American West, hoping for similarly dramatic economic consequences: 'The economic position of the Argentine might be compared with that of the United States some fifty years ago ... there is a very great demand for an industrious population, and the outlook for the willing worker who does not expect too much at first is perhaps as promising in Argentina as anywhere in the world.'[82] The control of workers, in other words, held out the possibility of expanding the League's reach into American territory and providing a basis for European-American economic cooperation. To encourage such settlement, the ILO encouraged the transfer of land to refugee settlers and the provision of higher wages than local workers normally received.

The ILO's work in service of the League's racialized global order went well beyond the provision of Latin American employment to stateless refugees from Europe. Originally assigned a responsibility to safeguard workers 'in countries other than their own', the organization now began to enshrine a deeply inequitable international approach to labour protection by creating legalized paths to the differentiated treatment of 'native' workers and European ones (whether locals or migrants) and ensuring states' and companies' capacities to dictate terms of employment in radically inequitable ways. Using language familiar to any defender of empire, its constitution declared that 'differences of climate, habits and customs' naturally would 'make strict uniformity in the conditions of labour difficult of immediate attainment'.[83] Following on this principle, then, the ILO constitution exempted colonial spaces from the necessity to follow its labour-related precepts, requiring them only when local conditions allowed. Concerned particularly with the provision of cheap employment across Africa, which the organization thought would almost certainly require the use of large numbers of migrants, it set up what it called a 'Native Labour Committee' in 1926 to set conditions for the control and organization of workers moving across borders in Africa, including in the mandatory states. Once again, this scheme was promoted as a technical rather than a political one: the commission would examine the question 'as thoroughly as possible from a technical point of view', with a guarantee that 'experts' would guide its outcomes.[84]

What did these experts decide? The resulting series of 'Native Labour Conventions' enshrined the principle of treating colonial workers differently from both metropolitan workers and colonial (European) settlers. Most

---

[82] 'Report on the Work for the Refugees', 127.
[83] *Constitution of the ILO*, Article 427. 'The Constitution of the International Labour Organisation', Treaty of Versailles Part XIII, 1919, available at Yale Avalon Project, https://avalon.law.yale.edu.
[84] Christopher Szabla, 'Entrenching Hierarchies in the Global Periphery: Migration, Development and the "Native" in ILO Legal Reform Efforts', *Melbourne Journal of International Law* 21/2 (2020), 334–72.

dramatically, they cited developmentalist arguments to allow for the continuation of unfree labour – lamenting the 'tragic contradiction' that such work was necessary for the civilizational improvement of the colonies and allowing its continuance subject to certain longer-term 'human guarantees'.[85] Under the terms of the ILO's Forced Labour Convention of 1930, forced labour was explicitly permitted for 'public purposes' – as a kind of necessary education for the native worker and a mode of development for the native state, legitimized by the constraints and regulations placed on it via legal internationalism.[86]

These agreements also enshrined a distinction between indigenous workers' rights and those of others. The Convention on Migration for Employment, for instance, guaranteed that migrant workers would receive the same treatment as domestic employees and outlawed misrepresentation for purposes of recruitment but explicitly exempted 'indigenous' workers from its protections. A separate convention dealing specifically with indigenous recruitment laid out conditions under which recruiters could operate without regulatory oversight and allowed authorities to enforce wage caps. It is worth noting that this system came under repeated bitter critique from activists for Black rights as they watched the League embed a nineteenth-century racial consciousness into the post-war legal system. As W.E.B. Du Bois put it in his role as Secretary of the Pan-African Congress as early as 1921,

> Labor and capital in England, France and America can never solve their problem as long as a similar and vastly greater problem of poverty and injustice marks the relations of the whiter and darker peoples. It is shameful, unreligious, unscientific and undemocratic that the estimate, which half the peoples of earth put on the other half, depends mainly on their ability to squeeze profit out of them.[87]

The ILO, then, sought to control and distribute workers across the colonial world for the benefit of, mainly, Western employers and investors, including states. As an institution, it used its authority to embed a racialized hierarchy of labour into a technocratic language of developmentalism, thereby ensuring that the legal and political distinctions it drew between the rights of workers in the metropole and the rights of workers in the colonies could be understood not as a political (or racial) distinction but as a scientifically determined approach to the thorny problem of how

---

[85] Daniel Maul, *Human Rights, Development and Decolonization – The International Labour Organization (ILO) 1940–1970* (Basingstoke: Palgrave Macmillan, 2012), 23–25.

[86] Ali Hammoudi, 'International Order and Racial Capitalism: The Standardization of "Free Labour" Exploitation in International Law', *Leiden Journal of International Law* 35/4 (2022), 779–99.

[87] W.E.B. Du Bois, 'To the World (Manifesto of the Second Pan-African Congress)', in A. Getachew and J. Pitts, eds., *W. E. B. Du Bois: International Thought* (Cambridge: Cambridge University Press, 2022), 55–65.

to develop the globe for a modern industrial age. This idea would have a long life; as legal scholar Christopher Szabla notes, it bears a strong resemblance to contemporary legal reforms promoted by institutions like the World Bank that claim to 'improve the "investor climate" of a country to attract foreign spending – ignoring the interest of other parties in the design of legal systems'.[88]

Direct Rule over Populations

We have looked at various manifestations of the League's various political framings for forcibly ordering people across the globe: border-making and migration, minority 'protection', refugee aid, and the regulation of global labour. But there were also places where the League actually served as direct ruler: notably, the 'Free City' of Danzig and the mandatory territory of the Saar.

Both these experiments in direct forms of international authority were established by the post-war peace treaties. The Free City of Danzig emerged as a mainly British-brokered deal intended to resolve the apparently intractable disconnect between Poland's historical and economic claims to the port city on the one hand and the political desires of its mainly German population on the other. A similar, if less direct, form of League oversight prevailed in Upper Silesia, where a special Allied regime claimed authority over the industrial region's economic life: railways, water, power, currencies, postal services, customs, and labour unions. The Treaty of Versailles outlined the conditions of Danzig's anomalous political existence as a semi-independent but externally monitored city-state, with its own parliament and senate, currency, and police force. It was to be 'protected' both by Poland, which retained a set of rights there (including the rights to represent the city in foreign affairs, to join with Danzig in a customs union, and to provide military defence should it prove necessary), and by the League of Nations, which had the right to appoint a resident High Commissioner who would (theoretically) settle disputes between Polish and German claims and guarantee the constitution, which it would vet and approve. ('It is particularly necessary,' wrote the League's Japanese representative in a report on Danzig, 'to see whether the Constitution of the Free City contains germs of disorder, inadequate government, anarchy or disregard for international obligations.'[89]) This form of international administration, which in practice concerned itself mainly with brokering disputes between Germany and Poland vis-à-vis the city, lasted until the Nazi invasion in the autumn of 1939. Legal scholars have pointed out that Danzig's reversion to Polish control at

---

[88] Szabla, 'Entrenching Hierarchies', 17.
[89] League of Nations, *Free City of Danzig: Report by His Excellency Viscount Ishii* (Geneva: League of Nations, 1920), 3.

Yalta, in the aftermath of the Second World War, was never formalized in any subsequent peace treaty and technically remains an informal arrangement.[90]

The League's rule over the Saar was still more direct, and considerably more extensive. Versailles enforced a notably different kind of mandate over the Saar than those in the Middle East and Africa: one in which the ruler was the League itself, for a period of fifteen years after which a plebiscite would be held to determine the territory's future. (In another example of removing economic questions from the political realm, the peacemakers separated the question of governing the Saar's population from access to its coal resources, which they gifted to the state of France.) The League's Governing Commission, charged with administering the territory, held unusually comprehensive powers; as the League itself noted, its commission's powers in some respects 'exceed[ed] those of an ordinary constitutional Government'. Despite claims of neutrality and stated commitments to 'self-determination' in a territory almost wholly inhabited by Germans, the commission was dominated by representatives of French interests, who worked to protect French commercial enterprises in the Saar and engaged in repeated expulsions of people suspected of German sympathies.[91] Objections to this French domination eventually resulted in the replacement of the president by a Canadian in 1926 and the subsequent withdrawal of French troops from the territory; but French domination of the Saar remained a feature of League administration, which even defenders acknowledged was an undemocratic one.[92] The plebiscite, when it was finally held in 1935, returned a near-total rejection of League governance and handed an overwhelming victory to advocates of reunification with Germany – an outcome that triggered a new refugee crisis and the League's decision, in accordance with its already-established practices vis-à-vis displacement and labour, to settle the Saar's fleeing refugees as workers on agricultural land in Paraguay.

The League's commitment to the control of populations across the globe manifested itself particularly in concerns around migration and labour, but also encompassed territorial border-drawing and, in some small, but notable, instances, the enforcement of direct internationalist rule over highly contested areas. Its population politics dovetailed in recognizable ways with its attempts

---

[90] Patrick Capps, Malcolm Evans, and Stratos V. Konstadinidis, *Asserting Jurisdiction: International and European Legal Perspectives* (London: Bloomsbury, 2003), 25.

[91] Nicolas Lemay-Hébert, 'Exploring the Effective Authority of International Administrations from the League of Nations to the United Nations', *Journal of Intervention and Statebuilding* 11/4 (2017), 473–74.

[92] Andrew Thomas Park, 'Administering the Administrators: The League of Nations and the Problem of International Territorial Administration in the Saar, 1919–1923', *International History Review* 44/3 (2022), 540–58.

to control other kinds of resources: land, currency, raw materials. In all these instances, the League's commitment to the idea of the national – with all the violence, expulsions, 'exchanges', and inequities that it implied – was made to serve the interests of the British, French, and (increasingly) American empires in ways that could outlast superficial, or even dramatic, forms of political change.

Perhaps the League's most important contribution to the population engineering of the interwar era was its insistence that populations could be the subject of technical expertise, and that their fates could – indeed should – be determined by 'scientific' processes rather than the vagaries of political engagement. As one American former member of the League Secretariat put it, its members were not 'representative of their countries [but] are there solely as experts in law, economics, history and administrative problems. So they can and do approach problems with a scientific detachment which is novel in international affairs'.[93] It was precisely through such claims of neutral technical expertise that the League and its various constituent agencies drew and enforced national borders along economic lines; processed refugees into low-wage colonial employers; declared minority petitions for equal treatment to be non-receivable; reinvented non-white colonial labourers as necessary fodder for state development; and deemed the interests of those being governed directly by the League basically irrelevant to its political arrangements in these contested territories. This insistence on the fundamentally technocratic nature of population politics (taken up by any number of states, UN agencies, and NGOs in the decades since the League's demise) is indisputably one of the League's longest-lasting legacies – indeed, arguably among its greatest triumphs. Remarkably, the League effectively made the near-total chaos of the post-war period serve its own purpose: to claim the greatest share possible of the world's resources and wealth for the ex-Allied imperial powers, largely through 'technical' modes of control that future political developments, however unforeseen, would be unable to alter.

2 Ordering Wealth

The League of Nations promised equality and institutionalized inequality. That process of stratification is the core theme of this study, and in no sphere of power was it more evident than in the organization of wealth. To appreciate how liberal orderers of the 1920s embedded economic inequalities in their reconstruction of

---

[93] Sarah Wambaugh, 'A New Kind of Frontier', *The Annals of the American Academy of Political and Social Science* 108/1 (1923), 174–77.

global capitalism, the place to begin is with the genesis of the League's economic mission.

The League emerged in a world of collapsing empires, mass displacement, waves of revolutionary and counter-revolutionary violence, hunger, protests, strikes, and a general clamouring for economic and political democracy and self-determination in the broken empires and colonies. The promise of a new order centred on a novel international institution sparked mass excitement and debate. During the war, blueprints for a league promising to transform global economic life appeared in campaign pamphlets and books penned by lawyers, journalists and politicians, some of whom influenced the first Anglo-American drafts of the Covenant.[94] Contributions from the international left ranged from Bolshevik denunciations of the project as a capitalist hoax to qualified support from reformist socialists, who saw in official plans for the League the makings of a future 'league of peoples' and, in the meantime, a useful international forum to pressure national governments for an 'immediate revision of those territorial, economic, and political clauses in the Treaties which violate the working class conception of a just and durable settlement'.[95] In November 1918 German enthusiasm for a league soared with the foundation of the Weimar Republic and the establishment of the 'German League for the League'. Drafted by the liberal law professor and politician Walther Schücking, Germany's draft proposal for a league of nations encapsulated the centre-left intellectual consensus around this new institution: the full membership of all sovereign states, the rule of law in international relations, the election of delegates to the league by national parliaments, and economic cooperation and equality.[96] But the peacemakers at Paris rejected German pitches as mere ploys to escape war reparations and profit from the rebuilding boom. Pressures from within the Allied camp to make the League a 'union of peoples' and a force for economic justice elicited essentially the same response.

Another impetus for a league to drive total economic transformation sprang from the success of the victors in building inter-Allied agencies to pool shipping, food, fuel, and industrial raw materials. If that machine could win a total war by suspending markets and seizing control of private assets, so ran the

---

[94] Jean-Michel Guieu, *Le rameau et le glaive: Les militants français pour la Société des Nations* (Paris: Presses de Sciences Po, 2008); Stephen Wertheim, 'The League of Nations: A retreat from international law?' *Journal of Global History* 7/2 (2012): 210–32; Kaiga, *Britain and the Intellectual Origins of the League*.

[95] Talbot Imlay, 'An Alternative International Relations: Socialists, Socialist Internationalism and the Post-War Order', in Peter Jackson, William Mulligan, Glenda Sluga, eds., *Peacemaking and International Order after the First World War* (Cambridge: Cambridge University Press, 2023), 313–36.

[96] Joachim Wintzer, *Deutschland und der Völkerbund 1918–1926* (Paderborn: Munchen, 2006), 138–59.

argument, then why not deploy it to engineer prosperity? Much of this speculation pivoted on the idea that the league could serve as a global economic command centre, directing scarce natural resources and food to promote worldwide growth and employment. A groundswell of opinion led by the international labour movement, women's organizations, peace campaigners, and some business lobbies called for natural resources to be distributed according to the principle 'nature made it; man should not monopolise it'.[97] Among the allies, Italian statesmen in particular campaigned to equip the League with the power to allocate commodities at low prices to resource-poor industrial nations with swelling populations. Many French officials also wanted to turn the economic war machine into a peacetime consortium to supercharge France's recovery and to hobble Germany's.

However, what officials labelled the 'socialist solution' – some sort of supranational body to govern the global economy – found little support among Western political and economic elites, who broadly regarded heavy-handed intrusions by inter-Allied agencies into national economic affairs as a necessary wartime evil but in peacetime an intolerable affront to national sovereignty, not to mention a threat to their own longer-term claims over resources, territory, and income. In July 1919 the Americans hastened the end of Allied economic cooperation by withdrawing from the Supreme Economic Council; but the lurch back towards market capitalism, and the reassertion of the autonomy of business and the sanctity of private property, was widespread across the Western world. It was one component of a counter-revolutionary strategy to contain the spread of communism in Europe and beyond. In 1922 the League capped the political drive to liberal globalization when it responded to an expert report analysing all the schemes touted to ease the problems of access to raw materials by endorsing the 'free trade solution'[98] – thereby staking out its own brand of liberal internationalism as an explicitly anti-communist (and, in practice, anti-Soviet) theory and practice.

In the end, then, the peacemakers did not object to the creation of new institutions to secure global capitalism – even when such institutions acquired the means to intrude in the internal affairs of theoretically sovereign states – so long as they did not meddle in the domestic affairs of the resource-rich empires and the United States, and so long as they acted to protect a highly stratified global economic and political order derived from nineteenth-century imperial theory and practice. The

---

[97] Karl Kapp, *Memorandum on the Efforts Made by the League of Nations towards a Solution of the Problem of Raw Materials* (Geneva: League of Nations, 1937), 36–41. The quote is from the British minister Arthur Balfour's summing up of Italy's position at the League Council.

[98] Mats Ingulstad, 'Regulating the Regulators: The League of Nations and the Problem of Raw Materials', in Andreas R.D. Sanders, Pål Thonstad Sandvik, and Espen Storli, eds., *The Political Economy of Resource Regulation: An International and Comparative History, 1850–2015* (Vancouver: UBC Press, 2019), 231–58.

emergence of novel internationalist agencies would thus follow a stratifying logic, legitimizing the sort of great-power interference that the pre-war empires had routinely deployed in their colonies and against weak states as a novel form of international economic regulation that conveniently reserved decision-making authority for themselves. As Jamie Martin puts it, 'the task of these institutions was to make their interventionist powers compatible with the legal fiction of sovereign equality and the mass politics of self-determination.'[99]

The breakthrough came in 1920 with the foundation of the League's Economic and Financial Organisation (EFO) by officials who had run the Allied war machine. Soon other multilateral agencies joined the fast-growing EFO to regulate trade and financial flows, working with the International Labour Organisation (ILO) and private entities (cartels, banks, think tanks, business lobbies) to consolidate common rules, practices, and statistical data and remake the global economy as a sphere of technocratic management. This form of capitalist internationalism enabled the United States to participate in economic policy making in Geneva around the shared public–private configuration of a stratified system of liberal globalization, without formal League membership.[100]

The Spoils of War and the Establishment of the Mandate System

The League's assertion of long-term control over resources and territories in what would become the 'mandate' territories (former holdings of the defeated Central powers) emerged, above all, out of the particularities of the Allies' wartime military occupations. From the Ottoman Empire to East Africa, the British and French armies took control of their opponents' territory with an eye to long-term possession. In a way, then, when the mandate system emerged it served less as an internationalization or re-legitimization of colonialism than as a way of rendering permanent already-established wartime claims over any number of financial and security interests in Middle Eastern, African, and Pacific territories.

The Allied occupations of Iraq and greater Syria were themselves not entirely new as expressions of British and French imperial ambition. Rather, they created a newly visible and newly physical form of what one scholar has called the 'mortgaging' of Ottoman territory during the long nineteenth century,[101] and they followed a long-extant pattern of securing, protecting, and expanding the

---

[99] Jamie Martin, *The Meddlers: Sovereignty, Empire, and the Birth of Global Economic Governance* (Cambridge MASS: University of Harvard Press, 2022), 9–10.
[100] Clavin, *Securing the World Economy;* Martin, *The Meddlers*.
[101] Matthew Jacobs, 'World War I: A War (and Peace?) for the Middle East', *Diplomatic History* 38/4 (2014), 776–85.

empires' extensive financial and commercial interests. In Mesopotamia, the first act of the (British) Indian Expeditionary Force was to capture the port city of Basra, thereby protecting the Anglo-Persian Oil Company's refinery operations at Abadan and ensuring imperial access to the Persian Gulf. As the invasion moved north towards Baghdad (very slowly, and enduring some serious reverses in fortune), a British military occupation staffed mainly by Indian soldiers was charged with figuring out how to bypass thinly stretched shipping lanes and establish a permanent extractive imperial economy across the whole of what would become Iraq, including the oil-rich northern areas around Mosul whose post-war disposition was not yet clear. To this end, the occupying administration established legal and judicial codes modelled on those of the Indian North-West Frontier, trying to encourage the emergence of recognized tribal units who could then serve as British clients and representatives. In Baghdad, finally occupied in 1917, a wartime civil administration claimed total control over food supplies, eventually implementing an 'Agricultural Development Scheme' in the Middle Euphrates region that sought a long-term and large-scale increase in the amount of land under cultivation. As the end of the war approached, the India Office told London that its goals should be to 'score as heavily as possible on the Tigris before the whistle blew'. This meant advancing quickly into the Mosul region to claim as much territory as possible, a goal actually accomplished only after the Armistice of Mudros had technically brought the Ottoman war to a close.[102] In other words, by the time the 'mandate' was negotiated, the territory that was to become Iraq had already spent some years under a thoroughgoing British imperial occupation of a distinctly extractive nature.

In Syria, Lebanon, and Palestine, too, the post-war mandates were applied to an already-occupied, already-divided, and already-governed landscape. This territory was a late addition to the wartime Allied portfolio, although the Anglo-French naval blockade that had been in place since 1914 had helped to reduce much of greater Syria, especially Mount Lebanon and Palestine, to a state of destitution and starvation.[103] The British capture of Jerusalem in December of 1917 brought an immediate bureaucratic presence in the form of the Occupied Enemy Territory Administration, even as the fighting continued and British troops conducted mostly unsuccessful raids across the Jordan River in an attempt to help Faysal capture Amman. In the autumn of 1918, Allenby and the Egyptian Expeditionary Force finally managed to break the Ottoman lines in the Galilee and move north to Aleppo, where they halted the campaign in late

---

[102] Kristian Coates Ulrichsen, 'The British Occupation of Mesopotamia, 1914–1922', *Journal of Strategic Studies* 30/2 (2007), 349–77.

[103] Melanie Tanelian, *The Charity of War: Famine, Humanitarian Aid, and World War I* (Oakland: University of California Press, 2017).

October, days before the armistice. The British and the French were already negotiating the specifics of their division of this territory and its resources. The eventual agreement they reached, involving a promise of a 25 per cent share of Mesopotamia's oil to France in return for its territorial withdrawal from Mosul, would hold until the nationalization of the Iraq Petroleum Company in 1972.[104]

In November, a British military edict apportioned the territory into distinct Occupied Enemy Territories. 'South' encompassed Palestine and fell under British military authority; 'West' and 'North', comprising Syria's coastline and Cilicia respectively, would be under French occupation; and an 'East' was assigned to an Arab administration under Faysal. It was not clear, here at the end of the war, that this would represent the final division of the spoils of war; but this immediate practical establishment of colonial administration, backed by occupying armies and overlaid with the familiar rhetorical justifications of small-nation rights and minority protections, would serve as the foundations of the mandate system in the Middle East. In other words, as the details of the line-drawing became clearer, these late-breaking 'internationalist' mandatory agreements mainly served to legitimize and formalize an already well-established system of military administration, derived from the specifics of the Allies' wartime occupations.

The same process unfolded in the African colonies that would eventually make up the second rank of the mandate system. In German East Africa, a British occupation took pieces of the territory throughout the war and administered them as an occupying military government. In 1916, in the midst of ongoing guerrilla warfare against German forces, the British resolved to begin running the area as a civilian administration – even assigning it a trade license 'as if such territory were a British Possession or Protectorate,' as the Colonial Office War Trade Department had it.[105] This civil–military blend featured a police force, a staffed civil administration, and plans to rebuild infrastructure and customs services. In 1922, then, when it became the new mandatory territory of Tanganyika – essentially, the old German East Africa minus Ruanda-Urundi, which was assigned to Belgium, and the Kionga Triangle, apportioned to Portuguese Mozambique – the territory already had a government whose administrative contours determined the specifics of the mandatory agreements, rather than the other way around.

The same trajectory developed in Togo and Cameroon, albeit featuring more public arguments between the British and the French. Here too, the emphasis was on economic control over resources, markets, and trade lanes; as the Banque Française de l'Afrique Equatoriale declared upon its production of

---

[104] Scazzieri, 'Britain, France, and Mesopotamian Oil', 25–45.
[105] Michael Callahan, *Mandates and Empire: The League of Nations and Africa* (Oxford: Oxford University Press, 1999), 14.

Figure 7 Colonial bureaucracies at work, before the formal accession of mandatory authority: stamp from Provisional French Mandate of Cameroon, 1921. Public domain.

plans in 1915 to locate a new office in Duala, Cameroon's main port, it was above all necessary to think of 'the economic victory which must follow the success of our arms'.[106] Here, the questions included not only raw materials but also the railways and the ports. The first partition agreement for Togo, in August of 1914, assigned Lomé and the railways to the British, to French discontent (see Figure 7). Cameroon, after conversations about some kind of 'condominium', mostly came under French provisional control in 1916, to British fury. In both instances, the French immediately set up colonial administrations with civilian elements that were clearly designed to outlast the war: health services, civil governments, agricultural development, and public infrastructure. In British Cameroon things were much the same, with large budgets to ensure the viability of roads, communications, food production, and police and security forces.

The major Allied powers were not the only ones to harbour the idea that their wartime occupations would be permanent spoils and act accordingly. German South West Africa – the site of the German-perpetrated Herero and Namaqua genocides a decade earlier – found itself occupied by South African troops, who were eventually given administrative responsibility for the technically British-mandated territory. Japan's occupation of German colonial possessions in the Marianas, Carolines, Marshall Islands, and Palau came early in the war, in October of 1914; the Japanese government

---

[106] Callahan, *Mandates and Empire*, 10.

immediately began running them as colonial possessions and negotiating to keep them more or less forever, signing a series of treaties with Britain and other Allies exchanging Japanese naval help in the Mediterranean for permanent suzerainty over what would become the South Seas Mandate.[107] Australia captured German New Guinea in 1914, a territory it intended to attach to Papua as an external Australian territory but which instead became the separate Territory of New Guinea under an Australian mandate. New Zealand's claims over German Samoa rested on its conquest and administration of the all-volunteer Samoa Expeditionary Force, which took Apia unchallenged in August of 1914 and left its commander to administer the island for the remainder of the war.

At the end of the war, then, the outlines of what would be dubbed the "mandate system" were already in place: a mix of military and civilian colonial administrations, enacted by occupying armies and based around Allied claims over not just territory but – more essentially – resources, markets, railways, and shipping lanes. The question in Paris, then, was not really how to defend these occupations, already coming under fire both literally and figuratively from nationalist claims to self-determination inspired (if not actually supported) by Wilson. The question, rather, was how to ensure that the underlying *conditions* of the mandate – Allied ownership of natural resources, control of labour and migration, unchallengeable control over ports and waterways, and (most of all) open access to markets – could be hardwired into any post-occupation government and made a permanent aspect of global politics, even if the claims of anticolonial nationalists someday won out in the political arena.

The Concept of Trusteeship and the Structures of the Mandates

It should surprise no one that the idea for the mandate system came, like the idea of the League more generally, from a white supremacist deeply devoted to an imperial ordering of the globe: Jan Smuts of the Union of South Africa. In his 1919 booklet *The League of Nations: A Practical Suggestion*, he proposed the basic idea of distributing territory to the victors through an imperial collective. In this iteration, the League would be 'clothed with the right of ultimate disposal', not only of the former German possessions but also of the 'peoples and territories formerly belonging to Russia, Austria-Hungary and Turkey'. It would be able to assign administrative responsibility to a state of its choosing, and retain the right of oversight and removal of a supervising power if necessary. The purpose of such a system? 'The mandatory state,' he declared, 'shall in

---

[107] Tze M. Loo, 'Islands for an Anxious Empire: Japan's Pacific Island Mandate', *American Historical Review* 124/5 (2019), 1699–1703.

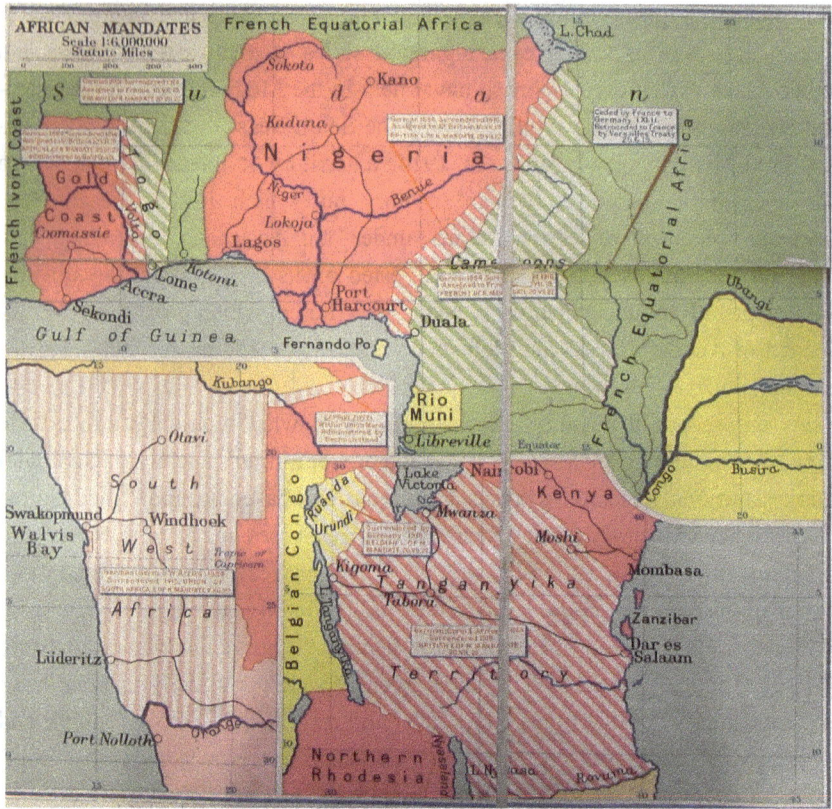

Figure 8 Mapping of colonial claims: inset from 'The League of Nations Map of the World', 1926, detailing the acquisition and disposition of the African mandates. League of Nations Archives.

each case be bound to maintain the policy of the open door, or equal economic opportunity for all, and shall form no military forces beyond the standard laid down by the league for purposes of internal police.'[108] In other words: the mandate system was to ensure the Allies' permanent control over the world's resources and markets, without altering the military balance of power among them. The long-term subjugation of local populations, who might well find themselves in objection, could be accomplished through the use of imperial 'policing' (see Figure 8).

Wilson found much to like in this vision, which corresponded to his own sense of the possibilities inherent in less schematic and more flexible systems of American control over spheres like Latin America. The nineteenth-century

---

[108] Jan Christiaan Smuts, *The League of Nations: A Practical Suggestion* (London: Hodder and Stoughton, 1918), 9–19.

Monroe Doctrine, which declared the western hemisphere to be the provenance of the United States, had been extended in 1904 with the so-called Roosevelt Corollary: Theodore Roosevelt's declaration, made in response to the European use of force to collect debts from Venezuela and other Latin American states, that the United States would act as an 'international police power' when necessary, 'to see the neighboring countries stable, orderly, and prosperous'.[109] Wilson, drawing on both Smuts and on these prior examples of an imperial 'ordering' not requiring actual occupation, had his own plan drawn up and printed in early 1919 (just days after meeting Smuts at a dinner arranged by Lloyd George) that both reflected Smuts' ideas and added some specifically American language about the open door. 'It shall be lawful for the League of Nations to delegate its authority, control, or administration of any such people or territory,' it ran, 'to some single State or organized agency which it may designate and appoint as its agent or mandatory.' Getting to the point,

> The Mandatary [sic] State or agency shall in all cases be bound and required to maintain the policy of the open door, or equal opportunity for all the signatories to this Covenant, in respect of the use and development of the economic resources of such people or territory. The mandatary State or agency shall in no case form or maintain any military or naval force in excess of definite standard laid down by the League itself for the purposes of internal police.[110]

As the negotiators fleshed out the idea of a mandate system, Wilson's and Smuts' shared concept of a kind of trusteeship increasingly seemed rhetorically useful, as did the idea of distinguishing among different types of mandate territories bearing different relationships with their governing states. In January of 1919, then, the Supreme Council settled that there would be three levels of mandate: 'A' mandates, reserved for the Arab provinces of the old Ottoman Empire, who were civilizationally advanced enough that 'their existence as independent nations can be provisionally recognized'; 'B' mandates, comprising most of the ex-German territories in Africa, who had reached only 'such a stage that the Mandatory must be responsible for the administration of the territory under conditions which will guarantee freedom of conscience and religion' and, of course, 'will also secure equal opportunities for the trade and commerce of other Members of the League'; and the 'C' mandates, in South West Africa and the Pacific, which were at such a low level of civilization that they could be

---

[109] Theodore Roosevelt's Annual Message to Congress for 1904 House Records HR 58A-K2, US National Archives, 33.
[110] Pitman Potter, 'Origins of the League of Nations', *American Political Science Review* 16/4 (1922), 563–83.

governed only 'as integral portions of [the Mandatory's] territory'.[111] It was in this context that perhaps the most infamous line in the League's covenant was generated: 'To those colonies and territories ... inhabited by peoples not yet able to stand by themselves under the strenuous conditions of the modem world, there should be applied the principle that the well-being and development of such peoples form a sacred trust of civilization.'[112]

Following on this, then, the mandate system's specificities began to emerge. Each territory to fall under the system would be labelled A, B, or C and assigned a mandatory overseer, which would govern it under the terms laid out in the mandate texts. These documents, which by and large were near-identical to one another (apart from that for Palestine, with its additional commitment to the cause of large-scale Jewish immigration with an eye to 'reconstituting' a Jewish national home), featured several themes specifying the nature of mandatory governance: in particular, 'protection' of distinct religious and ethnic communities, the right to use force to maintain public order, and the right to determine the territories' foreign relations and assure consular protection. Most central, though, were their material claims over these territories' economies: there would be no 'discrimination' against 'any State Member of the League of Nations (including companies incorporated under its laws) as compared with those of the Mandatory or of any foreign State in matters concerning taxation, commerce or navigation, the exercise of industries or professions, or in the treatment of merchant vessels or civil aircraft'.[113] The system as a whole would be overseen by the League's Permanent Mandates Commission: nine members appointed by the League Council, who would review annual reports submitted by the mandatory representatives and offer guidance to mandatory governments vis-à-vis their internationally defined obligations. A few years into the PMC's operations, it added a petitions system to permit the airing of grievances from the mandate territories that were deemed 'receivable' – that is, complaints that did not (among other things) challenge the fundamental legitimacy of any of the terms of the mandate itself.[114]

The Mandate System in Operation

This vision drew simultaneously on nineteenth-century European liberal imperialism, on American-style protectionism, and on particular aspects of

---

[111] League of Nations Covenant, Article 22, available at: https://www.ungeneva.org/en/about/league-of-nations/covenant.
[112] League of Nations Covenant, Article 22.
[113] This is from the Palestine mandate, but the language is nearly identical across the others.
[114] This was an especial issue for Palestine, where the mandate's explicit requirement to encourage mass Zionist immigration rendered the issue off-limits for petitioners.

contemporary liberal internationalism to make its case; and the system, as drawn out in these texts, indisputably provided a set of discursive concepts around which a wide variety of actors harbouring not a few serious disagreements could rally. But it is incorrect to say, as one historian does, that the Allies 'needed the mandates system, for it was the only defence against a charge of simple annexation'.[115] The mandates system was not, in its essence, particularly concerned with defending the Allies against charges of formal empire – a charge that mattered, once the Americans had withdrawn, only to small audiences in the metropole who could be persuaded that these occupations were essentially liberal ones. Its real benefits lay not in its rhetoric but in its practice: its flexible and multilateral governing arrangements, its deliberately vague temporal contours, its redefinition of wartime violence as internal security and policing, its impenetrable bureaucratic layers of petition and redress, its persistent turn to the 'technical' and the procedural as a response to protest. Taken as a whole, the mandate system was built to give the Allies time, space, and capacity to install their own permanent ownership over the most relevant pieces of the territories now up for grabs, and to recast said ownership as a scientific, even technocratic liberationist project focused around economic development, communications, free trade, control of trafficking, restriction of alcohol and drugs, and the provision of public health. If the system succeeded, as its architects hoped, in removing all such arenas from the realm of the political, then any eventual independence of these territories or other unforeseen change in their political status would make little difference in the ongoing disposition of their assets or their place on the global ladder.

The fundamental characteristic of the mandate system in practice turned out to be violence. Like other forms of colonial occupation, mandate powers found themselves relying on force or the threat of force – making use of already-extant military structures of occupation – to maintain or, in some case, to establish authority over their newly legalized possessions. In the Middle East, the British and the French bombed cities and villages from Beirut to Mosul in order to enforce the League's 'sacred trust'. In Mesopotamia, where a massive protest against British rule swept the country in 1920, Winston Churchill advocated the use of chemical weapons against northern Iraq's resistant villages.[116] That same year in Syria, the French deployed eighty thousand soldiers (mainly Algerian and Senegalese troops coming off France's recent defeat in Cilicia) to dismantle Faysal's constitutionalist experiment. In Palestine, where the

---

[115] Pedersen, *The Guardians*, 32.
[116] Martin Gilbert, *Winston S. Churchill* (London: Heinemann, 1976), companion volume 4, part 1, and R. Raymond M. Douglas, 'Did Britain Use Chemical Weapons in Mandatory Iraq?' *Journal of Modern History* 81/4 (2009), 859–87.

League's commitment to establish a 'Jewish National Home' with European Zionist settlers had given a special edge to local opposition to mandatory rule, the British forcibly removed the mayor of Jerusalem and subdued local protest against both British rule and Zionist immigration with air bombardment of civilians.

In all these cases, this initial brutality was a harbinger of things to come. Both the British and the French soon found that their newly acquired Middle Eastern possessions required an enormous amount of force to maintain. Another major rebellion consumed Syria from 1925 until 1927, during which the French bombing of Damascus flattened the city and killed tens of thousands of civilians (see Figure 9). The 'Great Arab Revolt' in Palestine, lasting for more than three years in the late 1930s, brought twenty thousand troops to keep colonial control over this tiniest of British possessions; by one estimate, British soldiers killed, deported, wounded, or arrested 10 per cent of the Palestinian Arab male population.[117] Iraq was so resistant to mandatory rule that the British, after putting down the initial protests with intensive bombing of civilians, put it under a form

Figure 9 Sacred trust of civilization? The aftermath of the French bombing of Damascus, 1925. Collection of the Massachusetts Historical Society.

---

[117] Rashid Khalidi, 'The Palestinians and 1948: The Underlying Causes of Failure', in Eugene Rogan and Avi Shlaim, eds., *The War for Palestine: Rewriting the History of 1948*, (Cambridge: Cambridge University Press, 2001), 12–36.

of client monarchy (tapping Faysal, recently under French bombardment in Syria, for the job of king). Even so, they continued to maintain colonial militias and an air force base to maintain their presence and protect their oil claims.

Mandate authorities across different territories made frequent use of minority 'protection' – an idea name-checked in the mandate documents – to exert political control over local populations. Through explicitly separatist border-drawing, refugee resettlement, migration policy, labour restrictions, colonial assemblies, and differential infrastructure development, Britain and France enforced a novel politics of difference across their new Middle Eastern possessions. Muslims, Christians, and Jews fell under different judicial regimes and differentiated wage scales within civil government. Communal franchises were introduced and enforced. In some places, the mandatory government presided over the construction and maintenance of single-community infrastructure – schools, hospitals, sometimes even roads.[118] The forcible occupation of the old Arab provinces, in other words, brought a violently enforced form of political sectarianism to the region designed specifically to create conflict and legitimize subsequent modes of mandatory mediation among apparently irreconcilably opposed local populations.[119]

Similar conditions of brutal occupation, and tactics of ethno-national division, adhered in the African mandates. In Togo, the border drawn between the British and the French mandates separated Ewe communities from one another and detached smaller populations from their historical hinterlands. The French practice of forcible Kabye settlement to provide cheap workers for French industrialization and agriculture likewise served to entrench new forms of ethno-national consciousness and internal opposition.[120] In British East Africa, an influx of German settlers seeking to restore some of their pre-war influence over what was now Tanganyika gave Donald Cameron, governor of the territory in the later 1920s, the opportunity to consolidate imperial rule around local divisions by bestowing administrative capacity on 'Native Authorities', a strategy that

---

[118] For Palestine, see Jacob Norris, *Land of Progress: Palestine in the Age of Colonial Development, 1905–1948* (Oxford: Oxford University Press, 2013); for Lebanon, see Elizabeth Thompson, *Colonial Citizens: Republican Rights, Paternal Privilege, and Gender in French Syria and Lebanon* (New York: Columbia University Press, 1999); for Iraq, see Toby Dodge, *Inventing Iraq, the Failure of Nation Building and a History Denied* (New York: Columbia University Press, 2005).

[119] Thompson, *Colonial Citizens*; Noah Haiduc-Dale, *Arab Christians in British Mandate Palestine: Communalism and Nationalism, 1917*–1948 (Edinburgh: Edinburgh University Press, 2013); Ussama Makdisi, *The Culture of Sectarianism: Community, History, and Violence in Nineteenth-Century Ottoman Lebanon* (Berkeley: University of California Press, 2000); Laura Robson, *Colonialism and Christianity in Mandate Palestine* (Austin: University of Texas Press, 2011), among others.

[120] Marius Kothor and Benjamin N. Lawrance, 'The History of Togo and the Togolese People', *African History Encyclopedia* (2023).

simultaneously established physical and political divisions within the governed population and systematized, centralized, and empowered the colonial state.[121] South West Africa, governed as a straightforward territorial addition to South Africa under its Class C mandate, witnessed the installation of a system of 'native reserves' that even the League understood as amounting to forced labour. The Bondelswarts rebellion of 1922 against such practices was, a contemporary observer reported, 'crushed with the use of considerable force, the natives being bombed by aircraft'.[122] In this case, a subsequent League investigation resulting in a slap on the wrist for South Africa demonstrated not so much League commitment to native interests as its clear differentiation between the rights of the dominant imperial powers to bomb their civilian charges in places like Iraq and Syria and the rights of a second-tier colonial authority to do the same.

Through all of this, the mandate system's mechanisms of oversight, mainly in the form of the PMC, provided a novel method not so much of airing or addressing the use of violence within the mandate system as encouraging and legitimizing them, not least by demonstrating over and over that peaceful protest or petitioning on the part of the oppressed would yield nothing.[123] The tiny percentage of petitions that reached a stage of active consideration were, generally, dismissed as unfounded or requiring no response; as one British official put it with respect to a protest about deportation and forced labour in French-controlled Lomé, in language that could serve to describe the League's general response to petitions from the mandates, 'it seems clear that the charges made by our dusky friends are not really substantial'.[124] It was a tactic calculated to make a show of procedural equity and justice for European audiences, while promoting fury and, eventually, physical retaliation on the ground amongst subjugated populations. Provoking such violence through the active discrediting of peaceful protest would in turn serve as further evidence for the necessity of the mandate system and the presence of civilizing mediators.

In the meantime, the work of investment and extraction went on. While the League made a show of protesting South Africa white settler violence and dispossession, its mandatory apparatus gave cover to the white acquisition of more and more land, the control of African labour, and an ever-increasing political portfolio for foreign-owned diamond mines. In Iraq, even as formal independence approached, the League-approved British presence cleared the way for a cabal of

---

[121] Callahan, *Mandates and Empire,* 137.
[122] E. Emmett, 'The Mandate over South-West Africa', *Journal of Comparative Legislation and International Law* 9/1 (1927), 120. Also Pedersen, *The Guardians,* chapter 4.
[123] This is also applicable to the minorities petition system, as pointed out in Cowan, 'Who's Afraid of Violent Language'.
[124] Callahan, *Mandates and Empires,* 139.

American, Dutch, French, and British (along with a single Armenian businessman by the name of Calouste Gulbenkian) to establish near-total control over Iraq's oil reserves. In Palestine, territory and infrastructure – including pipelines and railways – were consolidated under joint British-Zionist military protection, a deal sealed in the revolt and further institutionalized during the Second World War.[125] Precisely as its architects had imagined, all these structures of ownership and exploitation would long survive the formal demise of the mandate system.

Rescuing Liberal Capitalism

The League's mission as global capitalism's international rescue service began in the turbulent years of demobilization and reconstruction. A brief boom in 1920 yielded to a severe slump the following year. A global upsurge in class conflict stoked by inflation and hyperinflation threatened to tear the social order apart – not only of the defeated empires but also the victors and the nations that had remained neutral. During what in many places was called the 'red years', global capitalism appeared on the brink of collapse.

The counter-revolutionary bludgeon arrived in the form of a deflationary cycle in the spring of 1920, with the United States and Britain imposing the sternest policies of high interest rates and public expenditure cuts; Japan, France, and Italy adopting similar, though less severe, courses; and all of them driving a global contraction in prices.[126] Surging joblessness and falling wages strengthened the hand of employers against organized labour, while high interest rates protected wealth holders. Against this background of contracting structures of money and credit inflicting widespread misery and hardship, the League championed austerity and rejected wartime experiments in state control of production and resource allocation, not just as a practical approach but as a moral imperative.

The articulation of these doctrines occurred at the two first world economic conferences: Brussels in 1920 and Genoa in 1922. These League-organized events gathered bankers, economists, and statisticians from over thirty counties, including the United States. They are usually remembered as ineffectual because they yielded declarations of principles and practice rather than answers to the ongoing struggles over inter-Allied war debts and German reparation payments. But in fact, as historian Clara Mattei has shown, these declarations served to solidify the League's role as a producer and legitimizer of knowledge and technocracy, designed to render inequalities in wealth and political power as the natural outcome

---

[125] Dafnah Sharfman, *Palestine in the Second World War: Strategic Plans and Political Dilemmas, the Emergence of a New Middle East* (London: Sussex Academic Press, 2014), 5.

[126] Tooze, *The Deluge. The Deluge*: The Great War, America and the Remaking of the Global Order, 1916–1931 (London: Penguin Books, 2014), 353–62.

of scientific laws and apolitical regulations. Their leadership carefully depicted the conferences as 'scientific' gatherings, having the cohorts of eminent bankers, economists and statisticians attend as autonomous experts rather than national spokespersons, and producing a flood of standardized statistics and technical analysis on global trade, retail prices, commodity production, and public finances.[127]

The data-backed resolutions of the Brussels and Genoa conferences described an optimal world of balanced budgets, reduced tariffs, and a swift return to stable exchange rates via the resurrection of the gold standard. A restored monetary and trading system would push governments out of domestic and transnational markets and offer resource-poor nations access to raw materials and food supplies. Industries would be privatized to put them in hands of managers 'whose enterprise and experience are a far more potent instrument for the recuperation of the country' than the state. Budgetary rigour, financial orthodoxy, and the politics of demobilization went hand in hand with deep cuts to military budgets and an end to 'uneconomical' and 'artificial' practices such as food, fuel and transport subsidies shielding people from the market costs of these goods and services; reduced unemployment benefits would spur 'industry'. Balanced budgets had to come before social reform. The Brussels-Genoa technocracy implored long-suffering publics to 'work hard, live hard, and save hard'. Indeed, the resolutions actively blamed 'public opinion' for inflation and called on governments to educate people in the patriotic duty of austerity. The pursuit of fiscal, monetary and industrial austerity was thus not just as a technical device to correct fiscal profligacy: it was a civilizing mission, disciplining unruly workers and naïve populations unfortunately radicalized by the war.[128]

Enforcing the Brussels-Genoa Consensus

The makers of the Brussels-Genoa Consensus entertained worldmaking ambitions as far-reaching as those of the Washington Consensus of the 1990s. As one senior Genoa conference delegate put it, the austerity resolutions constituted 'a financial code not less important to the world today than was the civil code of Justinian'.[129] The League's opportunity to help implement the consensus arose in the context of the post-war financial and economic disorder in Central and

---

[127] Yann Decorzant, *La Société des Nations et la naissance d'une conception de la régulation économique internationale* (Brussels Peter Lang, 2011); Clara E. Mattei, 'The Guardians of Capitalism: International Consensus and the Technocratic Implementation of Austerity', *Journal of Law and Society* 44/1 (2017), 10–31.

[128] Mattei, 'The Guardians', 10–31; Mark Metzler, *Lever of Empire: The International Gold Standard and the Crisis of Liberalism in Prewar Japan* (Berkeley: University of California Press, 2006), 159–74, 199–209.

[129] Mattei, 'The Guardians', 21.

Eastern Europe. In particular, the impetus behind the establishment of the Economic and Financial Organisation at the Brussels Conference of 1920 stemmed from the mounting crisis of inflation and famine in defeated Austria.

The EFO's growing ranks of technicians pioneered the idea of conditional sovereign lending to enforce the 'civilizing' morality of austerity and to achieve lenders' geopolitical goals. 'The more prostrate a country is and the nearer to Bolshevism the more presumably it requires assistance,' observed one British statesmen, 'but the less likely is private enterprise to give it.'[130] Beginning with Austrian stabilization loan of 1923, over the next five years the League's financial organization spearheaded lending to Hungary, Greece, Danzig, Bulgaria, and Estonia: either to steady currencies and rebuild infrastructures, or to cover extraordinary expenses arising from inflows of refugees. Geneva had no funds of its own to disburse. It instead acted as an international facilitator for cash-strapped governments to access financial markets by liaising with the central banks of crediting countries, leveraging guarantees from borrowers and assuming the posture of a neutral arbiter. So effective was the League in this role of a 'money doctor' that the tag 'League loan' became a stamp of quality, inducing European and American investors to offer preferential rates.[131] By certifying the quality of a loan with impressive, standardized statistics, the League's EFO performed the function of a rating agency. As a fount of regular, reliable, and consistent economic data, moreover, the League was a crucial source of intelligence for the new American financial rating agencies such as Moody's Analyses Publishing.[132]

That American rating agencies and the League generated the same sort of 'scientific' knowledge to sanction the imposition of fiscal controls on nations is indicative of the twin ordering functions that League money doctoring and US 'dollar diplomacy' served. Both repurposed nineteenth-century financial imperialism, which the European empires had deployed to turn Egypt, the Ottomans, and Greece into fiscal protectorates, and which the Americans had likewise used in Dominican Republic, Nicaragua, Liberia, and Haiti.[133] That critics of Geneva's financial interventions in the centre of Europe decried them as the 'Ottomanization' and 'Tunisization' of 'civilised' states underscored that this precedent was not lost on anyone. Tellingly, Portuguese officials rejected League aid because of what it would imply about the legitimacy of its imperial

---

[130] Martin, *The Meddlers*, 64.
[131] Yann Decorzant and Michel Fouquin, 'Going Multilateral? Financial Markets' Access and the League of Nations Loans, 1923–8', *Economic History Review* 69/2 (2016), 653–78.
[132] Quentin Bruneau, *States and the Masters of Capital: Sovereign Lending, Old and New* (New York: Columbia University Press, 2022), 115–22.
[133] Emily S. Rosenberg, *Financial Missionaries to the World: The Politics and Culture of Dollar Diplomacy, 1900–1930* (Cambridge, MA: Harvard University Press, 1999).

mission. As one astute observer explained, if 'a nation confesses that it needs the economic tutelage of the League of Nations, what moral right ... can justify its possession of extensive colonies[?]'[134]

Austria's League-led rescue from hyperinflation, famine, and communism showed how financial support could pry open the domestic sphere of weak states to the demands of external experts, intent on enforcing the Brussels-Genoa consensus of balanced budgets, gold-backed money, and a small state. In 1922, in exchange for a League-sponsored stabilization loan, Vienna agreed to set up an autonomous central bank; implement severe austerity; privatize state industries; cut food subsidies, pensions, and other state benefits; slash the civil service; peg its currency to gold; and accept external financial oversight. Not surprisingly, the near-dictatorial supervision of Austrian finances in the implementation of retrenchment by the League's commissioners infuriated nationalists who raged at Austria's semi-colonial status. Yet the fact that the mandate to inflict pain at home came from abroad aided Austrian officials who wished to embrace the moral code of austerity, for they could claim that the only alternative to compliance was a spiral into a revolutionary abyss.[135] At the same time – with far-reaching consequences – the League's experiment in Austria and elsewhere endorsed technocratic authoritarianism as a potent instrument of modern governance and guarantor of socio-economic order. There was, of course, no direct causal path from the technocratic application of austerity in the 1920s under the League to the Austro-Fascist regimes of the 1930s. Still, the zeal with which Italy's liberal economists also applied that policy to peg lire to gold – to the applause of Western lenders and with the force of the Fascist regime – indicated to many where salvation would lie in the event of another financial meltdown.[136]

As diplomatic historians have long recognized, US non-membership of the League did not prevent the world's largest creditor from exercising its enormous financial leverage in Europe for political purposes.[137] (Wall Street banks, for instance, contributed 42 per cent of the loans in League-sponsored stabilization schemes.[138]) If anything, America's neither-in-nor-out status – a theme of this study – enhanced the capacity of the victors to shape the global order. The way

---

[134] Patricia Clavin, 'Men and Markets: Global Capital and the International Economy', in Glenda Sluga and Patricia Clavin, eds., *Internationalisms: A Twentieth-Century History* (Cambridge: Cambridge University Press, 2016), 97–101; Martin, *The Meddlers*, 91–98.

[135] Martin, *The Meddlers*, 76–91; Nathan Marcus, *Austrian Reconstruction and the Collapse of Global Finance, 1921–1931* (Cambridge, MA: Harvard University Press, 2018).

[136] Mattei, 'The Guardians', 16–31.

[137] For example, Melvyn Leffler, *The Elusive Quest: America's Pursuit of European Stability and French Security, 1919–1933* (Chapel Hill: University of North Carolina Press, 1979).

[138] Michel Fior, *Institution Globale Et Marchés Financiers: La Société Des Nations Face À La Reconstruction de l'Europe, 1918–1931* (Bern: Verlag Peter Lang, 2008), 284–93.

in which London and Washington broke the Franco-German deadlock after French and Belgium troops occupied the Ruhr in January 1923 to force Berlin to pay war reparations illustrates this point. As significant as the rest of East-central Europe was to stabilization, the Ruhr crisis, German hyperinflation, and armed rebellions by both the radical left and right against the Weimar Republic showed once and for all that the revival of liberal capitalism envisaged at Brussels and Genoa hinged on Germany's economic integration, a point driven home by the conclusion of the German–Soviet treaty of Rapallo in 1922. The geopolitical implications of the Franco-German standoff prompted Britain and the United States to intervene; and the League intervention in Austria provided the template.

With assistance of the Bank of England, the *Reichsbank* (the German central bank) contained hyperinflation. In 1924, a committee of international economic experts chaired by the US banker Charles Dawes negotiated a compromise on war reparations that would anchor Germany into the international monetary system. The Dawes Plan did not cut the 132 billion gold marks of reparations demanded by the victors in 1921, but it rescheduled payments to ease the financial burden. To restore Germany's creditworthiness and attract private (mostly dollar) loans, Berlin would peg the mark to gold, implement strict budget controls and austerity, accept external financial oversight, and reassert the autonomy of the Reichsbank. Under the Dawes Plan, Germany experienced a four-year recovery. Its gold and foreign currency reserves swelled. Still, neither the Dawes plan nor Weimar prosperity neutralized the impact of reparations and the imposition of foreign controls as sources of bitterness and radicalization in German politics. When the next reparations plan was negotiated in 1929 by another American banker, Owen Young, the negotiators doubled down on the strategy of turning political issues into 'technical' ones. Overt controls such as Allied oversight of German railways and the Reichsbank, French troops on the Rhine bridges, and the office of a General Agent for Reparations ended. Instead, to render the financial transaction commercial rather than political, Berlin would oversee its own payments to a non-governmental body, the new Bank for International Settlements located – in part to underscore the new institution's neutral status – in Basel, Switzerland.

The BIS was the logical culmination of a decade of multiple initiatives by a tacit coalition of the League, the most powerful central banks, and private financial institutions to realize the Brussels-Genoa dream of a stratified world capitalism thoroughly insulated from the realm of politics. The gold standard was the disciplining mechanism of that world. By the late 1920s most major currencies had been pegged to gold at fixed exchange rates in a monetary system operated by a rising number of mostly autonomous central banks, mandated to adjust national economies to respond to international flows of trade and capital.[139] In unifying world money to enable cross border flows of trade and investment, the top central bankers of the era, above all the American Benjamin Strong and Britain's Montague Norman, were not just moneymakers but world makers.[140] Leading private bankers like J.P. Morgan's Thomas Lamont regarded themselves as financial statesmen, planning and executing monetary stabilization campaigns in Europe and East Asia as part of a 'general effort to restore the civilized world'.[141]

The promise of climbing that civilizational hierarchy for credit, industrial development, and economic status was one of the most potent forces behind the informal alliance of League experts and bankers. The Soviet Union's adherence to the gold club and Japan's decade-long struggle to peg the yen to gold demonstrates how powerful that drive was. Lenin considered gold a ticket to the top of advanced economies. In 1922 the Soviet delegates arrived at Genoa with a plan to reform the League and its economic goals by, among other things, a return to gold-backed money, a fight against inflation, an equal distribution of industrial raw materials to help war-ravaged regions, and huge investments in worldwide transport networks and electrification. Moscow's plan was never formally tabled, but the Soviet Union did issue gold-backed rubles for international trade, for a moment of peaceful coexistence and limited domestic market reforms.[142] With an eye to importing Western technology to equip an industrial economy, Stalin too wished to keep the gold ruble. Arguably, the Soviet Union's turn to autarky in the late 1920s had more to do with balance of payment problems and plunging world commodity prices than an ideological rejection of markets.[143]

Beat Them or Join Them? The Implications of the League for Non-Members

For the secondary, tertiary, and further-down powers of this new world order, the League's increasingly consolidated control over the world's wealth (shared with the United States) begged the question of whether to try to oppose it or

---

[139] Barry Eichengreen and Andreas Kakridis, eds., *The Spread of the Modern Central Bank and Global Cooperation 1919–1939* (Cambridge: Cambridge University Press, 2023).

[140] Piet Clement, 'The Norman–Schacht Vision and Early Experience of the Bank for International Settlements, 1929–1933', in Barry Eichengreen and Andreas Kakridis, eds., *Modern Central Bank* 80–102; for the League's prominent efforts to rewrite trade law, see Madeleine Lynch Dungy, *Order and Rivalry: Rewriting the Rules of International Trade after the First World War* (Cambridge: Cambridge University Press, 2023).

[141] Metzler, *Lever of Empire*, 260.

[142] Ekaterina Pravilova, *The Ruble: A Political History* (Oxford: Oxford University Press, 2023); Irina Khormach, 'The "Kremlin" League of Nations Plan, 1920s', *Social Sciences* 39/4 (2008), 48–62.

[143] Oscar Sanchez-Sibony, 'Depression Stalinism: The Great Break Reconsidered', *Kritika: Explorations in Russian and Eurasian History* 15/1 (2014), 23–49.

partake in it. The case of Turkey, which after a lengthy period of uncertainty eventually became a member of the League in 1932, is instructive in suggesting the weighty consequences of both participation and non-participation in what those outside its purview fully understood to be a fundamentally coercive and exploitative system.

The emergence of the new Turkish Republic was one of the many ironic outcomes of the First World War: observers across what was now being called the Middle East reflected bitterly on the brutal occupation and subjugation of Arab populations who had assisted the Allied war effort, while the heirs to the defeated Ottomans successfully wrested a recognition of independence from their former enemies.[144] That independence, though, was hemmed about from all sides in ways that reflected a longer history of European intrusion into Ottoman territory and sovereignty: intrusion that had long taken humanitarian, liberal, and technical forms. The new nation's relationship with the League was marked, then, by a fairly clear-sighted understanding of its purposes and its mechanisms, informed by more than a century of interaction with European empire in its internationalist guise.

As historian Carolin Liebisch-Gümüş points out, Europe had long made use of internationalist organizations as venues for reinforcing the Ottoman Empire's simultaneous membership and distinctly non-equal status among the European powers.[145] For decades, Ottoman membership in organizations like the International Telegraph Union, the General Postal Union, the International Sanitary Conference, and the Red Cross (with the establishment of the parallel Red Crescent) opened up Ottoman territory to all kinds of European interventions – for instance, the European insistence on controlling the Ottoman Council of Health on the grounds that the empire broadly represented an epidemiological threat.[146] The Ottoman Public Debt Administration, a body of 'experts' hired from European creditor nations to collect taxes and distribute payment to private bondholders in the West, served as the most salient (and among the most resented) of these supposedly internationalizing institutions claiming to operate on non-political economic principles.[147] Further, the concept of external

---

[144] Hasan Kayali, *Imperial Resilience: The Great War's End, Ottoman Longevity, and Incidental Nations* (Redwood City: University of California Press, 2021).

[145] Caroline Liebisch-Gümüş, 'Intersecting Assymmetries: The Internationalization of Turkey in the 1920s and the Limits of the Postcolonial Approach', *Acto Universitatis Carolinae Studia Territorialia* 1 (2019), 13–41.

[146] On this point see especially Michael Christopher Low, *Imperial Mecca: Ottoman Arabia and the Indian Ocean Hajj* (New York: Columbia University Press, 2020).

[147] Murat Birdal, 'Fiscal Crisis and Foreign Borrowing in the Ottoman Empire: Historical and Contemporary Discourses and Debates', *Journal of European Economic History* 48/2 (2019), 83–107; Daniel A. Stolz, '"Impossible to Provide an Accurate Estimate": The Interested Calculation of the Ottoman Public Debt, 1875–1881', *British Journal for the History of*

'protections' for non-Muslims in the Ottoman sphere – a much-cited humanitarian/internationalist shibboleth from the second half of the nineteenth century – had repeatedly led to European incursions, including the military and territorial variety, into Ottoman lands.[148] By the time of the war, then, the Ottomans already had a long list of reasons to be suspicious of claims to some neutral internationalism serving the universalist causes of peace and progress.

The League did nothing in its earliest years to dispel these fears. Among its first acts was advocacy for the punitive Treaty of Sèvres, which proposed the dismemberment of Anatolia and portioned out the pieces to various Allied powers including Greece. When Mustafa Kemal's nationalist armies forced the treaty's abandonment and its reconsideration at Lausanne, the Allies asserted League supervision over minority rights in Turkish territory; forced a place for European legal advisors on Turkey's internal judicial reform team; placed the League as a supervisory power over civilian and military traffic in the Straits; and insisted on Turkey's assumption of a large part of the Ottoman debt under external enforcement. When, three years later, the League acted to assign the disputed (oil-rich) territory of Mosul to British-controlled Iraq above Turkish claims, it appeared that Mustafa Kemal's 1923 assessment had been confirmed: 'The League's error lies in that it sets up certain nations to rule, and other nations to be ruled.'[149]

And yet it was evident from an early date that Turkey could not join the global world order, even in a reduced capacity, without it. From the mid-1920s, the Kemalist government pursued a relationship with the League – particularly the ILO, which shared the regime's commitment to top-down, state-driven industrialization open to foreign investment within an anti-Bolshevik framework committed to limiting and controlling workers' power. By 1927 Turkey had agreed to participate in the World Economic Conference; in 1928 it participated in the Preparatory Commission for the Disarmament Conference; shortly thereafter it participated in the League's advisory committees on the opium trade (see Figure 10).[150] All these connections served to represent Turkey to the Western powers as part of a club of political players, a crucial step on the road to true sovereignty (and, for the moment, balanced out by a treaty relationship with the Soviet Union as well).

Science 55/4 (2022), 477–93; and Schilling and Aksakal, 'Turkey and the Division of the Ottoman Debt at Lausanne'.

[148] Michael A. Reynolds, *Shattering Empires: The Clash and Collapse of the Ottoman and Russian Empires* (Princeton: Princeton University Press, 2011).

[149] Liebisch-Gümüş, 'Intersecting Asymmetries', 13. On Mosul see Sarah Shields, 'Mosul, the Ottoman Legacy and the League of Nations', *International Journal of Contemporary Iraqi Studies* 3/2 (2009), 217–30, and Yucel Guclu, 'Turkey's Entrance into the League of Nations', *Middle Eastern Studies* 39/1 (2003), 186–206.

[150] Guclu, 'Turkey's Entrance', 194.

Figure 10 'Experts' at work: The League of Nations Opium Commission, 1921. League of Nations Archives.

Still, Kemalists remained anxious about the implications of participation in a system that they understood (correctly) as one designed to articulate and enforce global inequities. It was therefore crucial to insist on Turkey's position prior to its entrance; as Turkish nationalist Ziya Gokalp put it, 'what advantage will we gain by entering the League until we have definitively entered European civilization?'[151] The remaking of Turkey as a homogenous ethno-national state, especially, appeared key not just to its modernity but to its place in the hierarchy of nations, partially explaining the Kemalist commitment to the active and often violent ethnic remaking of Turkish citizenry.[152] Entrance to the League on Turkish terms (ideally, Turkish officials insisted, with representation on the Council) would represent the accomplishment of that place. In 1932, Turkey agreed to become a formal member of the League. In 1934, a Turkish

---

[151] Ziya Gökalp, *The Principles of Turkism* (Brill: Leiden, 1968), 47; also cited and discussed in Liebisch-Gümüş, 'Intersecting Assymmetries', 37.

[152] This understanding was by no means limited to Turkey. See Volker Prott, 'Assessing the "Paris System": Self-Determination and Ethnic Violence in Alsace-Lorraine and Asia Minor, 1919–23', in Emmanuel Dalle Mulle, Davide Rodogno, and Mona Bieling, eds., *Sovereignty, Nationalism, and the Quest for Homogeneity in Interwar Europe* (London: Bloomsbury Academic, 2023) 85–103.

representative took a seat as a non-permanent member of the Council, indicating its accession to a second tier of power within the organization.

In some respects, then, this wait-and-see attitude paid off. Turkey was never subject to any serious intervention from the Allies or the League with respect to its minorities (many of whom found themselves the targets of punitive regimes of exclusion, dispossession, and sometimes active persecution)[153] – an experience substantially different from Iraq, for instance, which even after nominal independence in 1932 found itself continually vulnerable to ongoing Allied intervention and, eventually, re-invasion, partly on the pretext of minority protection. But in other ways Turkey's involvement in the League solidified its second-rank economic status in ways that were impossible to challenge or reverse. Turkey's economic performance in the 1930s, far from the rapid development touted by the Kemalist government, did little more than match late Ottoman numbers in terms of production and industrialization.[154] In the political realm, attempts to use its influence at the League to put together a Mediterranean pact to resist Italian expansionism in Ethiopia failed in the face of great power determination to negotiate only amongst themselves.[155] Turkey's main diplomatic victory as a League member, during the few years the organization had left, was its reclaiming of a degree of military control over the Straits in 1936. But even here, in keeping with long-standing principles of imperial internationalism, it had to recommit to 'recognise and affirm the principle of freedom of passage and navigation by sea in the Straits'. It is an agreement that is still in effect today.[156]

Turkey had managed to join the game on reasonably favourable terms; but even so, it found itself playing by rules that were increasingly determined in places where the rise of independent nation-states, the successes of anti-colonial movements, even the dissolution of the League itself mattered not at all. The League's structuring of the world's money, resources, and channels of exchange was designed to survive the disbanding of the imperial system by removing

---

[153] Lerna Ekmekcioglu, 'Republic of Paradox: The League of Nations Minority Protection Regime and the New Turkey's Step-Citizens', *International Journal of Middle East Studies* 46/4 (2014), 657–79; see also Carolin Liebisch-Gümüş, 'Embedded Turkification: Nation Building and Violence within the Framework of the League of Nations 1919–1937', *International Journal of Middle East Studies* 52/2 (2020), 229–44.

[154] Isik Ozel, 'An Evaluation of the Economic Performance of Turkey in the 1930s Based on Late-Ottoman Economy', *New Perspectives on Turkey* 23 (2000), 125–46.

[155] Dilek Barlas, 'Turkish Diplomacy in the Balkans and the Mediterranean: Opportunities and Limits for Middle-Power Activism in the 1930s', *Journal of Contemporary History* 40/3 (2005), 441–64.

[156] League of Nations Treaty Series, 'Convention Regarding the Regime of the Straits, Signed at Montreaux, 20 July 1936'.

questions of money from the political realm, putting it instead in the hands of bankers and technocrats and humanitarians whose backing by the world's most powerful militaries was not immediately evident.

With the arguable exception of Germany, one of the notable features of this system was that the League's construction of hierarchy generally took little account of its participants' status as winners or losers of the war. Rather, its main architects engaged in a ruthlessly self-interested demarcation of influence, measured in terms of degrees of access to raw materials, entry to global markets, territorial access, and control over currencies and spending. The League's liberal rhetoric was among the least important aspects of this system, which persuaded mainly by doing: convincing powers like Turkey, for instance, that they could not enter into the global system at all without submitting to the League's (and by extension the Allies') various forms of intervention, control, and influence. Once within the system, of course, the promise of economic advancement would prove essentially illusory; participants could move up in the world only insofar as the broader hierarchy was preserved. The assessment, shared by Britain and Turkey, of the latter as a 'small great power'[157] was the most Turkey (and any number of other secondary actors) could hope for: a degree of sharing in the spoils of empire, in return for quiet cooperation with a system of permanent global inequity. It was a bargain that would survive not only the dissolution of the League but also the disintegration of the empires that had built it.

3 Ordering War

Scholars are unanimous: As the cornerstone of world peace and security, the League of Nations failed. The Geneva experiment taught Cold War–era realists that peace came only through strength; many blamed the Western powers for failing to operate the machinery of collective security in the crisis-ridden 1930s. Later revisionists echoed that line, while finding new virtue in the League's pioneering of 'peace' in fields that appeared freshly relevant after the fall of the Berlin Wall: global health, economic development, multilateral arbitration. Across generations, these scholars shared a narrative of liberalism as a noble creed imperilled by implacable foes bent on replacing order with anarchy:[158] a consensus that overlooked – perhaps even actively ignored – how the League served as the centrepiece of broader ordering of the world designed above all to

---

[157] See Barlas, 'Turkish Diplomacy in the Balkans and the Mediterranean', 441–64, and Brock Millman, 'Turkish Foreign and Strategic Policy 1934–42', *Middle Eastern Studies* 31/3 (1995), 483–508, for British and Turkish (respectively) formulations of this phrase.

[158] Samuel Moyn, *Liberalism against Itself: Cold War Intellectuals and the Making of Our Times* (New Haven: Yale University Press, 2023).

promote the permanent geopolitical supremacy of the principal victors: an effort that in the end proved supremely successful.

The emergence of a League-centred vision for a world configured to sustain liberal empires, and inhibit threats to them from any quarter, should come as no surprise. The First World War, after all, erupted after four decades of violent imperial expansion, great-power rivalry, and ever-escalating arms races. Before 1914, the competitive geopolitical implications of these trends haunted statesmen, industrialists, and intellectuals worried about a coming division of the globe into a few 'giant powers'. And indeed, as historians like Edward Barbier have outlined, the pre-war era marked the advent of forms of military/economic strength based on the mastery of 'global vertical frontiers' of fossil fuels, minerals, and iron ores.[159] In another historian's account, this 'territorialisation of industrial capitalism' linking 'an industrial centre to a resource-rich periphery via an imperial state now served as the primary model for a sovereign unit in world politics.[160]

After 1914, this expectation of a world dominated by a few antagonistic economic blocs profoundly shaped war aims – and not just in Europe.[161] In 1915 Japan issued twenty-one demands to China that, had they been fully accepted, would have turned China into a Japanese protectorate and preferential economic zone.[162] Faced with the looming prospect of a world closing to American exports, the Wilson administration reasserted American dominance in the western hemisphere in two ways: US businesses began to supplant European traders in Latin America, and the US naval and merchant fleets grew. In June 1916, at the inter-Allied economic conference in Paris, the British and the French planned – with the reluctant assent of resource-poor Japan and Italy and industrially backward Russia – to exploit their maritime supremacy to control global trade, especially in food and raw materials, and throttle the German economy during and after the military conflict. To compete in global markets, Berlin planned to organize Europe into a German-controlled commercial zone, or *Mitteleuropa*, and in the spring of 1918 briefly achieved some success when it imposed punitive peace terms on Russia and Romania.[163]

---

[159] Edward B. Barbier, *Scarcity and Frontiers: How Economies Have Developed Through Natural Resource Exploitation* (Cambridge: Cambridge University Press, 2011).

[160] Sven Beckert, 'American Danger: United States Empire, Eurafrica, and the Territorialization of Industrial Capitalism, 1870–1950', *American Historical Review* 122/4 (2017), 1137–70.

[161] Georges-Henri Soutou, *L'Or et le sang: Les buts de guerre économiques de la Première Guerre mondiale* (Paris Fayard, 1989).

[162] Metzler, *Lever of Empire*, 92–96.

[163] Ragnhild Fiebig-von Hase and Maria Sturm, 'Die transatlantischen Wirtschaftsbeziehungen in der Nachkriegsplanung Deutschlands, der alliierten Westmächte und der USA, 1914–1917', *Militärgeschichtliche Mitteilungen* 52/1 (1993), 1–34.

Historians often understand Allied war aims and diplomacy at the Paris Peace Conference of 1919–20 as a clash between nineteenth-century competitive power politics and a new diplomacy of liberal internationalism, with the former advocated chiefly by French and British officials and the latter championed by the US president. Specific interpretations vary, but historians generally agree that the battle between the nationalistic impulses of vengeful victors and the utopian aspirations of liberal internationalists yielded a muddled peace, one in which neither old-style power politics nor Wilson's vision of an international society amplifying the 'moral force' of world public opinion could triumph; and the League of Nations embodied that muddle.[164] The Geneva dream promised lasting peace but bound none of its makers to enforce collective security, a fatal flaw that was compounded by the refusal of the US Senate to vote for American membership of the League in March 1920.[165]

In fact, though, the League-centred order that emerged in the 1920s was not some unstable mixture of power politics and utopianism; it was the early handiwork of a remarkably adaptable deliberative process of liberal world ordering that successfully synthesized powerful global trends to preserve and enshrine the material advantages of the liberal empires. In particular, far from being inimical to strategic considerations, liberal internationalism in the form of the League proved itself remarkably adept at configuring the trappings of modern warfare to secure overwhelming advantages for its main showrunners. Its toolkit included legal-institutional barriers to total war; efforts to redefine war to license imperial 'policing'; and a careful distribution of war-making potential to ensure that the Atlantic powers would enter any future total war with all the material and maritime advantages that had won it for them the first time. Indeed, throughout the twentieth century, advocates of a liberal world order embraced with very little difficulty all kinds of advanced technologies of mass destruction, from bombers to atomic bombs, as 'machines of peace'.[166] A deeper look into the ordering of the world in the 1920s reveals a similar synthesis, one which responded innovatively and flexibly to the new political economy of industrial-age total war and its threat to liberal capitalist imperial metropoles.

It is time, then, to revisit the League's actual relationship with war and with the ever-present question of 'security'. And to grasp how that process unfolded

---

[164] See for instance Peter Jackson and William Mulligan, 'The Crisis of Power Politics' in Peter Jackson, William Mulligan, Glenda Sluga, eds., *Peacemaking and International Order after the First World War* (Cambridge: Cambridge University Press, 2023), 114–50.

[165] Stephen Wertheim, 'The League That Wasn't: American Designs for a Legalist-Sanctionist League of Nations and the Intellectual Origins of International Organization, 1914–1920', *Diplomatic History* 35/5 (2011), 797–836.

[166] Zaidi, *Technological Internationalism*, chapter 1.

to secure a preponderance of power for the Atlantic victors and inhibit great power threats, it is important to look beyond the disputes among the leading protagonists at the Paris Peace Conference – as substantial and bitter as they were – and instead focus on outcomes.

An Atlantic Security Alliance?

In his exhaustive study of the subject, Georges-Henri Soutou concluded that Allied economic war aims survived the quarrelling in Paris intact. Germany was territorially, economically, and politically hobbled, and the main beneficiaries of the new map of Europe were new states that would work to contain Germany, Austria, and Hungary. This delineation gave Czechoslovakia defensible frontiers, a large industrial base, and a wealth in coal that paid dividends in settling its territorial claims.[167] Romania, an Allied power, doubled in size and population. Poland acquired former Prussian territory and access to the Baltic, and the port city of Danzig became a ward of Geneva. Based on the resolutions of the June 1916 Paris Economic Conference, the Treaty of Versailles imposed punitive terms on German trade, intellectual property rights, and foreign assets.[168] The allies imposed similar discriminatory commercial conditions on Germany's allies, and blocked Austria from forming a customs and political union with Germany. More broadly, the German, Austro-Hungarian, Ottoman, and Russian empires lay in ruins, and the only first-class navies on the world's oceans flew the flags of the victors, underscoring their control of global food, raw materials, and money. The French and British empires expanded to all-time territorial maximums with the incorporation of the colonial territories of the German and Ottoman empires, and Article 21 of the Covenant of the League of Nations affirmed American predominance in the western hemisphere.

In other words, the conflict had placed the Atlantic victors in (very staggered) pole positions to attain the geopolitical status of 'giant powers' and offered them the scope to permanently embed that outcome in international politics. The question was, how? As Western officials well knew, the war had not been won simply by making more guns and fielding larger forces than their foes. The Allies had prevailed by exploiting a half-century of British-centred globalization to direct money, shipping, food, and raw materials to their war economies and starve their adversaries of critical resources.[169] Some officials, especially among the budding cohorts of international technocrats who had built the inter-Allied system to pool resources and blockade enemies, saw a league of nations

---

[167] Piahanau, 'Each Wagon of Coal', 86–116. [168] Soutou, *L'Or et le sang*, 840–51.
[169] Theo Balderston, 'Industrial Mobilization and War Economies', in John Horne, ed., *A Companion to World War I: Volume One* (Chichester: Wiley-Blackwell, 2010), 217–33.

as a way to legitimize the continuance of that triumphant economic war machine in peacetime, now as a driver of reconstruction and an enforcer of order.

The most far-reaching and detailed plan for a formal economic security regime to unite the West came from the French economy minister Étienne Clémentel. His initial plan centred on implementing the June 1916 inter-Allied conference resolutions via the formation of a transatlantic economic bloc. This 'Atlantic community' would uphold the European settlement by controlling raw material supplies and the cost of sea transport, and, using the same levers, propel France's industrial and commercial recovery beyond that of Germany's.[170] With far less detail but no less world-making ambition, the influential British geographer and politician Halford Mackinder urged the peacemakers to form the League as a league of democracies with an overtly geopolitical mission. According to him, unless the Atlantic victors strengthened the small states that lay between Berlin and Moscow, one or both as allies would inevitably mobilize Eurasia's vast raw materials, populations, and industrial potential in the service of a world tyranny.[171]

Why did these collective security projects, which some consider as forerunners to NATO, the Marshall Plan, and the European Union, not solidify into an equally strategically robust League? For one thing, historians have argued, the fall of the Germanic empires removed the June 1916 rationale behind a permanent Western economic bloc for waging trade war if, as many expected, the military conflict ended in stalemate. Subsequently, the entry of the United States into an anti-German coalition tilted the policy debate between two competing forms of economic liberalism: in the end, the return to pre-war laissez-faire liberalism favoured by most Anglo-American officials won against the state-centric 'organized liberalism' endorsed by leading French economic planners.[172] While this explanation appears complete, it is not. The first step to a full explanation requires abandoning an often-unacknowledged Cold War model for security institutions, and instead appreciating the artful strategies that lay behind the League's schemes: for in the 1920s liberal world orderers, quite deliberately, sought to make the economic-military supremacy of the Atlantic victors informal and latent rather than conspicuous and burdensome.

As the centrepiece of that project, the League served to revive liberal capitalist globalization as the engine of the geopolitical power of the Atlantic

---

[170] Peter Jackson, *Beyond the Balance of Power: France and the Politics of National Security in the Era of the First World War* (Cambridge: Cambridge University Press, 2013), 247–62.

[171] Halford John Mackinder, *Democratic Ideals and Reality: A Study in the Politics of Reconstruction* (London: Constable, 1919).

[172] Georges-Henri Soutou, '"Le libéralisme organisé": un programme national et international', in Marie Christine Kessler and Guy Rousseau, eds., *Etienne Clémentel (1864–1936): Politique Et Action Publique Sous la Troisieme Republique* (Brussels: Peter Lang, 2018), 355–74.

victors. As we saw in section two, Geneva reconstructed the international monetary system, spread the liberal creed of a small state, free markets, and austerity, and shifted wartime preferential trade networks towards a carefully modified global system of free trade. The League presented the inequitable trade rules imposed on the defeated powers as a necessary aspect of the pursuit of globalization, holding out the promise that their producers would eventually benefit from reliable raw material, fuel, and food imports as well as access to foreign markets for their exports. Conveniently, of course, those short-term punitive conditions also permitted the victors to protect strategic industries and, especially, allowed France to recover shielded from German commercial competition. 'Technical' experts in Geneva devised other general regulations regarding the opening of world markets that preserved further specific exemptions beneficial to the victors.[173]

The importance of international expertise in engineering the global economy revealed not just the League's central purpose but its central practice. British and US officials rejected the idea of an Atlantic bloc partly because they worried that any conspicuous instrument of a forever trade war would keep European hatreds burning. A formal security organization would also require that the governmental and intergovernmental agencies of war economy continue into peacetime, just when liberal capitalism itself was threatened by revolutionaries who wanted to use such agencies to build global socialism. A general return to laissez-faire liberalism, instead, would de-politicize global economic reconstruction, rendering touchy political issues as merely technical problems and fully empowering decentralized transnational networks of liberal capitalist hegemony like the gold standard, with its web of independent central banks, 'money doctors', credit ratings, cartels, and markets.[174] The manoeuvre of de-politicizing questions of hierarchy and inequality, or insulating them from direct political challenge by embedding them in complex deliberative international procedures (such as making German-Austrian unification a matter for the League Council, where the French would veto it),[175] was a defining practice of liberal ordering. It is telling that both an arch-critic of the League, the German jurist Carl Schmitt, and a Geneva booster, the British political theorist Alfred Zimmern, agreed that the structuring power of the League of Nations lay in its ability to make the evolving liberalized world of growing interdependence look neutral, natural, and inescapable. 'The League,' Zimmern observed, 'was becoming, in a sense and to a degree of which this could be said of no national centre of government, a point of convergence between Knowledge and Power.'[176]

---

[173] Dungy, *Order and Rivalry*, 94–116.   [174] Mattei, *The Capital Order*.
[175] Jackson, *Beyond the Balance of Power*, 242–43.
[176] Stephen Legg, *Spatiality, Sovereignty and Carl Schmitt: Geographies of the Nomos* (London: Routledge, 2011), 119.

That convergence of knowledge and power never reached completion. Hardwiring global economics and security to fix the imperial and geopolitical outcome of the war and to inhibit challenges to the new order was an elaborate and open-ended process: one of official and unofficial international negotiations, norm cultivation (or as it was called at the time 'moral disarmament'), and the mobilization of transnational networks of League-minded activists, scholars, policy entrepreneurs, and technical experts of all kinds, based in both private and public institutions. That the chief victors stood to benefit enormously from this process did not preclude bitter quarrels among them about German reparations, Allied war debts, the inviolability of Europe's western frontiers (especially after the British–American security pacts offered to France in 1919 in exchange for its abandonment of the Rhineland fell through), and attempts to secure competitive advantage in trade or natural resources. What made these disputes so fierce was precisely the knowledge that the liberalizing world bound their fates together. Not surprisingly, the big three dealt with particularly divisive issues among them such as a formal commitment to military aid in Western Europe by shunting them into long-drawn-out and inconclusive legal-technical debates about draft protocols.[177] The most noticeable gap between them, US non-membership of the League, was hardly a gap at all because of the deep involvement of Americans in the organization's technical work or in initiatives that paralleled the Geneva agenda. As Schmitt put it in 1928, with respect to the League the Americans mastered a peculiar state of 'absence and presence'.[178] The League-centred liberal international security order, then, took shape in the 1920s in subtle ways: strategies of economic sanctions and integration alongside the promotion of carefully delimited forms of disarmament and what contemporaries called the 'outlawry' of war.

Sanctions and Interdependence

The most profound and enduring liberal internationalist innovation of the 1920s was the legal-conceptual transformation of wartime blockade into an international instrument of 'peace' enforcement. Clémentel's formal economic alliance of transatlantic victors did not materialize, but Wilson and other top Paris peacemakers did write economic sanctions into Article 16 of the League Covenant as the Geneva organization's primary coercive device. Nicholas Mulder argues that the magnitude of that change has been overlooked. Blockade starved to death nearly

---

[177] Zara Steiner, *The Lights That Failed: European International History 1919–1933* (Oxford: Oxford University Press, 2005), 349–456.
[178] Schmitt, *Positionen und Begriffe*, 100–110.

a million people during the war and traumatized countless more, and of course also violated stated pre-1914 liberal values like the sanctity of private property and freedom of the seas. Its use against Russian and Hungarian communists and all manner of populations in the Eastern Mediterranean sparked furious public debate about the ethics of punishing subjects to discipline rulers, as well as about the embrace of targeted humanitarian relief as the palliative conceptual flipside to blockade. Against this background, the League's formal legitimization of economic sanctions as a peacetime coercive weapon of choice is indeed striking.

In the 1920s the possibility that the League Council might enlist member states to sanction Covenant breakers spawned a growing network of legal, economic, and military experts – across Geneva, national governments, and private institutions of all kinds – engaged in studying how to sever flows of food, fuel, and raw materials, ration the trade of neutral states, seize property, make pre-emptive purchases, and offer victims of attack some kind of logistical support. As Mulder points out, Article 16 was intended mainly to serve as a general deterrent; 'no nation would destroy itself in these civilized times by inviting such a penalty,' predicted one British statesman.[179] Although in theory all League members would be called upon to enforce sanctions, the burden would, of course, actually fall to those with the largest navies and the capacity to break global supply chains. That this meant the victors was lost on no one, especially in places that had just felt the grinding force of the Allied blockades. As a truncheon of imperial policing, the deterrent worked. In 1921 the sanctions threat convinced Belgrade to abandon its invasion of Albania. In 1925 it persuaded Athens that triggering war with Bulgaria was a bad idea. No wonder, then, that efforts by the top arms-exporting states, including the United States, to prevent anti-colonial movements from acquiring small arms and regulate the military balance among arms-importing nations triggered intense resistance from small states.[180]

The perception that sanctions served to discipline small 'semi-civilized' states was reinforced when in August 1923 Italian warships bombarded the Greek island of Corfu in retaliation for the murder of an Italian army officer.[181] Often seen as the League's first failure to check fascism, the resolution of the Corfu crisis instead illustrated how the embryonic new order worked to bind subaltern colonial empires to it through economic dependence. Advocates of liberal internationalism anticipated that accelerated economic globalization would make isolation from the world economy intolerable and create an interdependence so

---

[179] Mulder, *The Economic Weapon*, 111.
[180] David R. Stone, 'Imperialism and Sovereignty: The League of Nations' Drive to Control the Global Arms Trade', *Journal of Contemporary History* 35/2 (2000), 213–30.
[181] Anthony Di Iorio, 'Continuity and Change in Italian Foreign Policy under Fascism: A Re-examination of the Corfu Crisis of 1923', *International History Review* (2024), 1–18.

tight as to make military action to enforce order largely unnecessary. Mussolini's attack on Corfu was dealt with outside of the League, because the ambitions of Italian liberal imperialists had already been curtailed at Paris in 1919 and geopolitically checked by a growing alliance between France and Yugoslavia.[182] During the war Italy had built powerful heavy industries reliant on imports of coal, scrap metal, and minerals, and on foreign markets for exports. It is hardly surprising then that the Fascist regime took a sharp globalizing turn in the 1920s by imposing austerity and pegging the lire to gold, a feat only made possible by large British and American loans and remarkably generous terms for the restructuring of Italian war debts.[183] Rather than being hostile to Geneva, the Italian state and its political elites were stalwarts of the new organization because of the inflated political status and influence Geneva bestowed on Rome.[184]

Japan's integration in the new order as a recently industrialized nation with a very slim natural resource base, and reliant on foreign markets for raw materials, followed a pattern similar to Italy's. Japan's economic war aims in China were scaled back when London and Washington supported China's objections, and at the Paris Peace Conference, its representatives failed to win formal recognition of racial equality to enable greater migration. Still, Japan embedded itself as a pillar of the liberal order; the empire embraced Geneva, arms control, and parliamentary politics.[185] As its economy stabilized in the 1920s, Japan's liberal elites, with the encouragement of American and British financial experts, imposed austerity and strove to fix the yen to gold as the monetary pivot of industrial growth at home and a commercial empire in East Asia.

Sanctions appealed to the peacemakers as a corrective to the turn-of-the-century precept that economic globalization made war between advanced industrial powers impossible. Before 1914 few had anticipated how European arms races would grow into the mobilization of entire economies and empires to fight a long war that ended only with the fall of empires. That the Western powers waged total war with efficiency and success did little to alleviate the horror of liberal elites at how the totalizing dynamic of industrial age war tore apart the fabric of the late nineteenth-century world: limited governments became sprawling interventionist bureaucracies, the steadily integrating world

---

[182] Stefano Marcuzzi, *Britain and Italy in the Era of the Great War: Defending and Forging Empires* (Cambridge: Cambridge University Press, 2020).

[183] Roland Sarti, 'Mussolini and the Italian Industrial Leadership in the Battle of the Lira 1925–1927', *Past & Present*, 47/1 (1970), 97–112; Marianna Astore and Michele Fratianni, '"We Can't Pay": How Italy Dealt with War Debts after World War I', *Financial History Review* 26/2 (2019), 197–222.

[184] Enrica Costa Bona, *L'Italia e la Società Delle Nazioni* (Padua: Nuova Cultura, 2004).

[185] Frederick R. Dickinson, *World War I and the Triumph of a New Japan, 1919–1930* (Cambridge: Cambridge University Press, 2013).

of gold-backed money and transnational markets fractured, and war socialism and mass regimentation prevailed.[186] For the liberal world orderers of the 1920s, nothing was more crucial than preventing arms competition from escalating into total war: hence the centrality of the new practice of sanctions, combined with 'disarmament'.

Disarmament

To understand how that goal was pursued, and the role of the League of Nations in its implementation, it is important to appreciate that it was not a pacifist endeavour. As the violence in their empires amply showed, liberal elites by no means rejected the use of force outright.[187] Rather, liberal strategists envisaged a world in which they could wield advanced weaponry against the disruptive forces of 'barbarism' without endangering cosmopolitan capitalism. David Edgerton describes this combination of a universalistic crusading creed, a predilection for high-tech capital-intensive firepower, and an acute awareness of the role of political economy as the wellspring of modern power as 'liberal militarism'.[188] The goal of 1920s disarmament, then, was not to end conflict; it was to make the world safe for this liberal militarism (see Figure 11).

Studies of disarmament usually begin in 1919–20 with the insertion of Article 8 into the League Covenant, which urged the world to disarm to a level consistent with collective security and imposed treaty limits on the size and type of armed forces the defeated enemy states could field. However, arguably the most successful form of disarmament took place in the realm of economic reconstruction. As we saw in Section 2, the resolutions of the League-sponsored 1920 Brussels and 1922 Genoa economic conferences proclaimed a new world of balanced budgets, markets unbound from wartime controls, revived flows of trade and investment across borders, and a return to stable exchange rates by resurrecting the gold standard. Budgetary rigour and monetary orthodoxy went hand in hand with calls for governments to slash military budgets and to dismantle war economies. Of course, under the popular pressure to release millions of men in uniform back into civilian life and to wind down unneeded munitions industries,

---

[186] Jay Winter, ed., *The Cambridge History of the First World War: Volume 2 the State* (Cambridge: Cambridge University Press, 2014).

[187] Martin Thomas, 'The Challenge of an Absent Peace in the French and British Empires after 1919', in Peter Jackson, William Mulligan, Glenda Sluga, eds., *Peacemaking and International Order after the First World War* (Cambridge: Cambridge University Press, 2023), 151–75; Rebecca Herman, 'Latin America and US Global Governance', in Brooke L. Blower and Andrew Preston, eds., *The Cambridge History of America and the World* (Cambridge: Cambridge University Press, 2022), 153–173.

[188] David Edgerton, *Warfare State: Britain, 1920–1970* (Cambridge: Cambridge University Press, 2006).

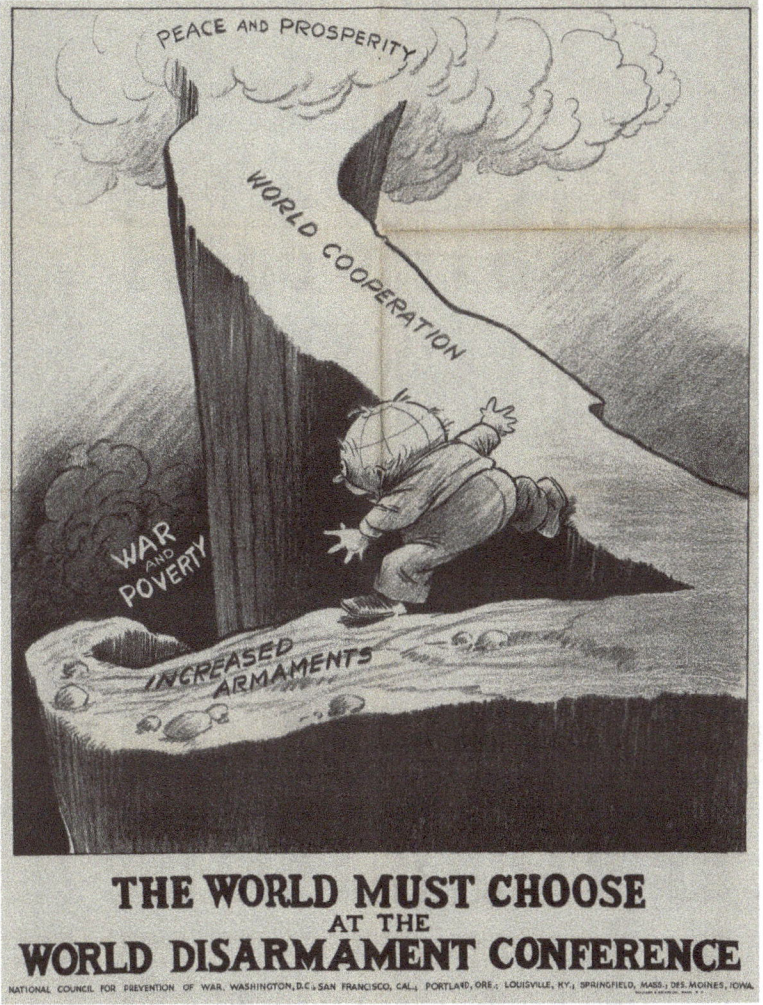

Figure 11 An uncritical (even propagandistic) view of disarmament: poster published by the National Council for Prevention of War, 1932. League of Nations Archives.

military budgets would have shrunk anyway. But the key point was that the return to gold in the 1920s placed a financial constraint on the size of armed forces a government could maintain and erected a major barrier to exceeding it through economic autarky, particularly for great powers that relied on imports of industrial raw materials, food, and fuel. What has been usually understood as disarmament was an outcome of binding national budgets with fetters of gold.

In fact, the term 'disarmament' was itself misleading. The decade and a half of negotiation over the size and structure of armies, navies, and air forces and over

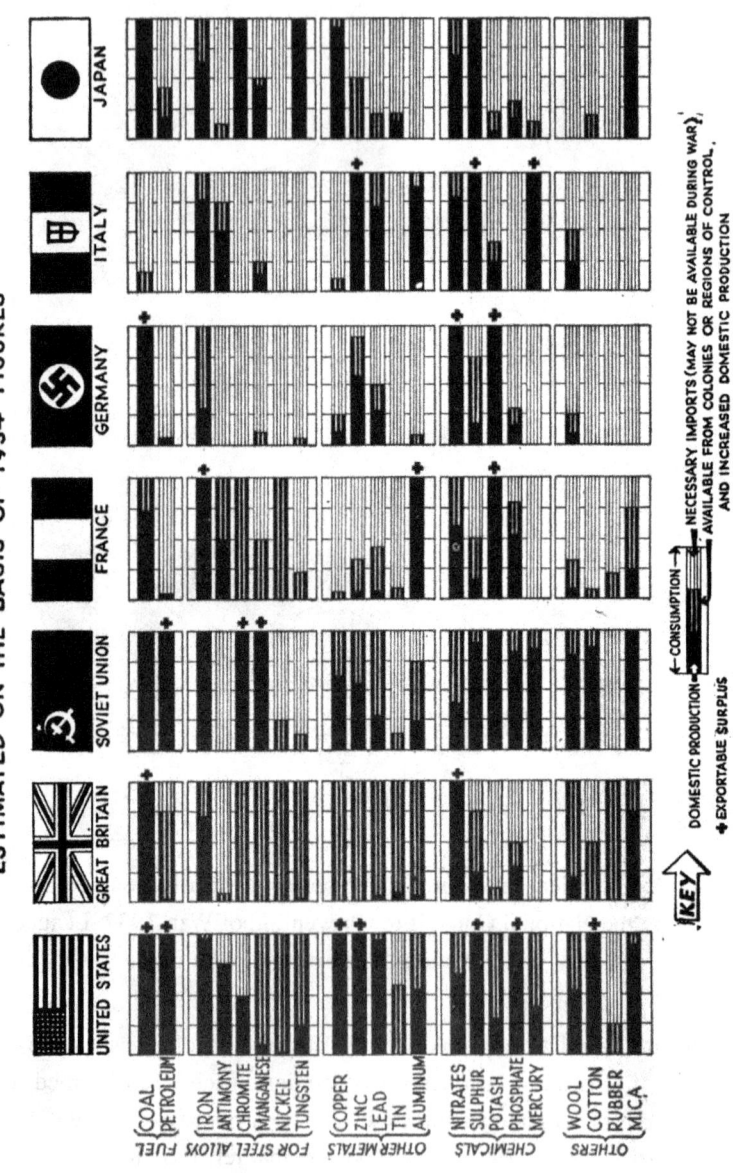

Figure 12 Chart showing distribution of access to raw materials before the war, published in Brooks Emeny, *Mainsprings of World Politics* (Foreign Policy Association-Headline Series, 1943). Public domain.

the characteristics of weapons such as battleships and aircraft actually represented a form of arms control: a method of fixing the distribution and minimizing the cost of peacetime forces among the leading military powers, not an attempt to abolish militaries and war altogether. That this approach advantaged wealthy economies that could maintain naval shipyards, artillery foundries, and aviation firms through state contracts and exports, as well as support the development of sonar, tanks, and aircraft carrier–based aviation, was abundantly clear to everyone involved. In the years that Germany remained disarmed and the Soviet Union began to rebuild its economy, arms control ratified the hierarchy of naval power and elaborated ways to regulate the time-consuming construction of the costliest weapons of the period (big-gun warships), thereby constructing a bloodless method of resolving disputes among the victors (see Figures 12 & 13).

It is also striking how successfully the cause of disarmament accommodated the 'absence and presence' of the United States in what was after all one of the League's principal tasks. A series of naval treaties began with the Washington Conference of 1921–22 and stretched into the mid-1930s. Among the agreements concluded at Washington, a five-power treaty fixed the total tonnage of battleships and aircraft carriers for British, the US, Japanese, French, and Italian navies in ratios of 5:5:3:1.75:1.75. It also set maximum tonnages and gun sizes for each type of warship and, with some exceptions, delayed the construction of new battleships for ten years. In the narrative of League disarmament, for which many politicians would claim credit, such naval ratios exemplified how 'technical' expertise could be applied to shrink arsenals and slash spending. In fact, of course, the ratios served above all to freeze the naval balance and establish the victors' long-term control of oceanic commerce. They also channelled potentially serious interstate disputes into ostensibly technical debates about how to balance different geo-strategic needs for patrolling colonial empires and defending regional hegemonies. For instance, US and British experts worked on 'yardsticks' and other arcane formulas to settle a bitter quarrel between the two navies over the size and number of cruisers in each fleet. For anyone familiar with the notionally deterministic maths of big-gun sea battles, the ratios also proclaimed a racial-civilizational hierarchy of victors; after all, the largest fleets would always win. That the United States, Britain, and France could in various combinations sink the Japanese or Italian battle fleets and starve the resource-poor island/peninsula nations into submission was a logic of naval warfare that admirals everywhere understood. The benefits, of course, did not flow only one way. For Japanese and Italian admirals, the tonnage ratios offered them symbolic status in world affairs and maximum tonnages above what would otherwise have been economically and competitively sustainable. Finally, naval arms control, by categorizing ships and defining their key features, imposed

Figure 13 Naval arms control upheld the supremacy of the principal victors at minimum cost: Royal Navy battleships of the Atlantic fleet in line, 17 January 1930. Alamy, by permission.

a symmetry of force structure on all the world's navies that again advantaged big fleets. This explains, among other things, why in the 1930s Britain strove to incorporate Germany and Soviet Union in qualitative naval arms control; it served as a means to channel their warship expansion programmes in the least dangerous direction.[189]

The big-gun ship captain's adage that small fleets make great targets, and the fact that naval power rested on large and technologically advanced industries, explains why the Washington treaty signatories had few qualms about the League's inconclusive attempts to extend the ratios to small states at the 1924 Rome Naval Conference.[190] Naval arms control remained an exclusive sphere for the Washington powers, while the League devoted itself to technocratic

---

[189] Joseph Maiolo, 'Naval Armaments Competition between the Two World Wars', in Thomas Mahnken, Joseph Maiolo, and David Stevenson, eds., *Arms Races in International Politics: From the Nineteenth to the Twenty-First Century* (Oxford: Oxford University Press, 2016), 93–114.

[190] Gerard Silverlock, 'British Disarmament Policy and the Rome Naval Conference, 1924', *War in History* 10/2 (2003), 184–205.

solutions to problems such as fulfilling the pledge that the peacemakers had made to Berlin either to disarm to their level or incorporate Germany (which joined the League in 1926) into a functioning Geneva-centric system of land, air, and sea arms control. When they ridicule the ten years of mind-boggling technical debate in the League's Preparatory Commission for the General Disarmament Conference of 1932–34, historians are missing the point – which was precisely to turn contentious political issues, like military imbalances and whether Britain would automatically come to France's aid if attacked by Germany, into open-ended study of how to calculate military strength, count defence spending, and decide whether certain weapons could be classified as uniquely offensive and others essentially defensive. In other words, it served to neutralize what political scientists would later call the 'security dilemma', the proposition that in seeking their own safety governments unintentionally induce a sense of fear in others and set in train a competitive cycle of self-defeating security seeking.[191] When in 1932 the German government insisted on the Allies fulfilling their 1919 pledge to disarm or permit Germany to rearm, they responded by granting Berlin equality of status and once again attempted to shunt the issue of how that theoretical equality should be put into practice into technical studies and negotiations among 'experts'.[192] The idea that science offered apolitical solutions to the menace of global warfare was a powerful one.[193]

At the World Disarmament Conference, French officials proved particularly adept at leveraging the widespread belief that the threat posed by new instruments of war, particularly aviation, demanded that the League should command its own armed forces to police the globe. The most radical schemes called for Geneva to control all forms of aviation, including civil transport. French officials had no expectation that the idea would be realized, but thought it might help them force London and Washington to commit to defending France's eastern frontier in exchange for authorizing a limited-controlled German arms build-up. The excitement that the idea of a heavily armed Geneva provoked in liberal internationalist circles was telling. It was obvious that the cadres, machines, and industrial infrastructure for this police force would come from the scientifically advanced nations – a prospect that fed on and electrified images of racial utopias, including the idea that a unification of transatlantic world would usher in perpetual peace.[194] H.G. Wells' *The Shape of Things to*

---

[191] The classic statement is John Hertz, 'Idealist Internationalism and the Security Dilemma', *World Politics* 2/2 (1950), 157–80.

[192] Andrew Webster, *Strange Allies: Britain, France and the Dilemmas of Disarmament and Security, 1929–1933* (London: Routledge, 2020), 307–26.

[193] For instance: Victor Lefebure, *Scientific Disarmament* (New York: MacMillan, 1931).

[194] Duncan Bell, 'Before the Democratic Peace: Racial Utopianism, Empire and the Abolition of War', *European Journal of International Relations* 203 (2014): 647–70.

Figure 14 The league of airmen restore peace over the forces of barbarism unleashed by total war: still from Alexander Korda's film version of H.G. Wells' The Shape of Things to Come, 1936. Alamy, by permission.

Come (1933), which told the tale of a league of airmen who rescue the world from a total war-induced age of barbarism, captured powerful cultural currents about how the science of destruction was running ahead of an internationally organized peace, with salvation depending on decisive action by the enlightened. For proponents of a League air police (and typical of liberal militarism), the logic of those cultural currents authorized the most extreme violence, including the bombing of civilians, to defend 'civilization' (see Figure 14).[195]

Critics of disarmament pointed out that Geneva's preoccupation with establishing collective security by setting measures for technical features of weapons and the size of national forces turned international attention away from decisive military and geopolitical inequalities in such key areas as industrial potential and natural resources. After all, they pointed out, the assembly-line logic of total war had erased the dividing line between soldiers and civilians, machine-guns and machine tools, armour and plate and iron ore. What strategists called 'war potential' encompassed people, factories, transport networks, infrastructure, agriculture, electricity generation, and raw materials. Even the League's

---

[195] Zaidi, *Technological Internationalism*, 74–96.

Armaments Yearbooks (published from Geneva between 1926 and 1940) acknowledged this inflated definition of what constituted armament by including national statistics on industrial production and the consumption of raw materials such as coal, oil, minerals, metals, chemicals, and fibres.[196]

The critics were right. The omission of war potential from the disarmament talks was deliberate: one part of a broad strategy of reversing the escalatory cycle that had produced a world of total war, and restoring the normative-legal boundary between war and peace, private and public, civilian and military. In section two we saw how the Paris peacemakers also rejected 'socialist' solutions to inequalities of raw material stocks and markets, mounting a stubborn defence of the liberal principle of national and imperial ownership of resources and arguing that a return to functioning commodity markets would ultimately solve what was a trade problem. Here, just as in earlier in the 1920s when the victors implemented their economic war aims, retained their dominance in known sources of commercially exploitable fossil fuels and minerals, and commanded the world's oceans, the object of general disarmament was to make their preponderance in war making power latent rather than apparent. For many who had supported some kind of internationalization, the danger of the market solution to raw material inequalities lay in the widely accepted view that a scramble for territory, resources, and markets had caused a great war and might well do so again. For many political commentators, moreover, the war's outcome confirmed the geopolitical predication that the globe would be dominated by a few imperial blocs, with the Atlantic victors achieving a head start and the resource-rich Soviet Union, if it ever industrialized, appearing as a contender as well. The task of removing the political sting from these geopolitical projections and their potential for causing resource-related conflict fell to League of Nations.

During the 1920s, Geneva's trade experts worked through international business networks to ease access to national and colonial commodity producers, make markets legible with reliable statistics, lower trade barriers, and rationalize production and stabilize prices through League sanctioned commodity cartels.[197] Friction over natural resources, though, continued. Among the victors, tensions over oil, copper, and rubber made headline news with rumours of transatlantic trade wars. How to diagnose and solve 'the raw material problem', as contemporaries often called it, produced a deluge of academic analysis. Geologists studied the geographic distribution of mineral wealth to uncover

---

[196] For example: G. Hosono, 'The "War Potential"', in Norman Angell, Francis Delaisi, John F.C. Fuller, et al., eds., *What Would Be the Character of a New War?* (London: King, 1933), 118–207.

[197] Ingulstad, 'Regulating the Regulators', 231–58.

how industrialization and developed supply chains structured hierarchies in world politics between producers and consumers and haves and have nots.[198] Geopolitically minded authors, meanwhile, studied the role of natural resources in world politics by compiling tables of nationally controlled resources to depict a static situation of decisive advantages and potentially fatal scarcities in the event of economic sanctions or, if it came to it, total war.[199] Liberal economists and international trade officials, by contrast, presented the problem as a dynamic movement of prices and volumes of trade in raw materials: complex market mechanisms, in need of expert fine-tuning. Properly functioning global markets, they affirmed, structured a world of peace-promoting interdependencies and competitive trade advantages that benefitted everyone, for no nation – not even the continent-spanning United States, or the territorially giant Soviet Union – was truly self-sufficient.[200]

In the mid-1920s, however, League experts discovered that while the production of food, raw materials, and finished goods eventually overtook the pre-war years, trade remained stubbornly flat owing to growing protectionism – a trend that slowed the development of poor nations with rising populations, and aggravated tensions across national borders. To strengthen the case for freer trade at the 1927 World Economic Conference, the League appointed the geographer André Siegfried and the economist M. Julius Bonn to study the economic causes of war. Both scholars explained raw material conflicts as a security dilemma: in other words, a psychological predicament rather than a political one. 'It is not so much the use or abuse of monopolistic power,' wrote Bonn, 'as the fear of such possible use and abuse which are influencing the attitude of nations living in less-favoured circumstances towards their more fortunate neighbours.' 'In certain cases,' Siegfried added, 'this fear may become a veritable obsession.' This psychological malfunction required technical fixes to induce confidence in the machinery of world trade, such as a 'code of international economic hospitality'.[201] From this perspective, the equal opportunities afforded by the dynamic mechanisms of global trade made the geopolitical advantages of a static distribution of mobilizable resources for total war irrelevant. But while these two spheres

---

[198] Andrea Westermann, 'Geology and World Politics: Mineral Resource Appraisals as Tools of Geopolitical Calculation, 1919–1939', *Historical Social Research* 40/2 (2015), 151–73.

[199] For an example, see J. Edward Ely and Brooks Emeny, *The Strategy of Raw Materials: A Study of America in Peace and War* (New York: MacMillan, 1934).

[200] Lionel Birch, *The Demand for Colonies: Territorial Expansion, Over-Population, and Raw Materials* (London League of Nations Union, 1936) and 'Report of the Committee for the Study of the Problem of Raw Materials', 8 September 1937 (Official No: A.27.1937.II.B.).

[201] Moritz Julius Bonn and André Siegfried, 'League of Nations Economic Tendencies Affecting the Peace of the World', *The Annals of the American Academy of Political and Social Science* 150 (July 1930), 192–219.

were routinely framed in opposition to each other, the liberal order of the 1920s increasingly enabled the Atlantic victors to reap the benefits of free-market globalization without surrendering their own strategic potential to take control of much of the earth's sources of food, fuel, and industrial raw materials in the event of war.[202]

Redefining War

The reframing of the belligerent blockade as a peacetime tool of international action in the League of Nations Covenant pointed to one of most expansive features of liberal ordering: the legal-conceptual drive to render total war both illegal and unthinkable, and to legalize and legitimize imperial-regional policing of an often-brutal kind.

One of the innovations of the League Covenant was to reinvent armed conflict as a public problem instead of a private matter between belligerents. It delegitimized wars between states that had not first exhausted all the pacific remedies such as arbitration and then observed a three-month cooling-off period. Collective wars for the restoration of peace could occur, though, and the sovereign right of self-defence remained a fact of international life. 'Aggression', or a single state using force without League authorization, was illegal. As Kirsten Sellars points out, the use of the word 'aggression' signalled that nations would not just be punished for losing wars, but for starting them. In principle, members of the League could not declare themselves neutral in the face of criminal aggression; indeed, the very idea of neutrality drew sharp rebukes from liberal internationalists who saw an iron wall of blockade as the most effective 'peaceful' weapon of collective coercion. In practice, though, neutrality remained a legal possibility because governments could opt out of enforcing Article 16. To limit opt-outs by vulnerable states, pro-League activists lobbied Geneva to adopt a new convention allowing members to offer each other economic support to make sanctions work and help victims of aggression.[203]

Of course, much turned on the question of how to define aggression and identify when it became a tripwire for collective action. Like general disarmament, the negotiation of a definition of aggression in draft protocols pivoted on

---

[202] As David Edgerton argues, the resource advantages of the anti-Axis coalition combined with blockade and offensive action became a self-reinforcing strategic advantage: David Edgerton, 'Controlling Resources: Coal, Iron Ore and Oil in the Second World War', in Michael Geyer and Adam Tooze, eds., *The Cambridge History of the Second World War: Vol.* 3 (Cambridge: Cambridge University Press, 2015), 122–48.

[203] Mulder, *The Economic Weapon*, 156–75; Kirsten Sellars, *'Crimes against Peace' and International Law* (Cambridge: Cambridge University Press, 2015), 7–16.

the disagreement between London and Paris about the former's readiness to defend the Paris peace treaties. And, like later disputes over NATO's Article V (the gold standard of security commitments), the Franco-British argument revolved around the question of what latitude signatories should exercise in deciding whether and how to respond in a crisis.[204] To an extent, that impasse was broken by the western pact signed at Locarno in October 1925, which declared the inviolability of the Franco-German frontier and in which Britain undertook to serve as one of the guarantors of the agreement against 'flagrant violations'. This interactive legal-conceptual process, though, continued to churn out definitions of illegal wars and what sort of military actions short of war would be permissible in a League-secured world.

The most significant outcome of this sort of self-interested rulemaking was the Kellogg-Briand Pact of 1928, which originated in an attempt by the French Foreign Minister Aristide Briand formally to connect the United States to Locarno via a bilateral treaty repudiating war. The US Secretary of State Frank Kellogg counter-proposed a multilateral pact committing signatories to 'condemn recourse to war for the solution of international controversies, and renounce it as an instrument of national policy in their relations with one another'.[205] Sixty-seven governments adhered to the Kellogg-Briand Pact, including Germany, Italy, Japan, and the Soviet Union, and many hailed the pact as a milestone. However, the reservations that Paris, Washington, and London placed on the treaty expanded the concept of self-defence and redefined the meaning of war in ways that enabled and legitimized liberal militarist practices of global imperial policing.[206]

Although Kellogg did not make the point explicitly in public lest he provoke a backlash in the region, he asserted that the American conception of self-defence included the enforcement of the Monroe doctrine. He also avoided the term 'aggression' in the pact because he did not want to appear to be offering Geneva the authority to make legal pronouncements about the American use of force or to intervene on behalf of Latin American states. Britain likewise claimed that the right of self-defence enveloped its empire and other strategically critical regions, which according to the Foreign Office included all possible routes to India. Britain's Foreign Secretary Austin Chamberlain added that self-defence encompassed 'actions short of war' – in other words, that any threat to the Suez Canal would prompt British intervention in quasi-sovereign Egypt. The irony that a pact to outlaw war effectively endorsed a 'British Monroe

---

[204] Timothy A. Sayle, *Enduring Alliance: A History of NATO and the Postwar Global Order* (Ithaca: Cornell University Press, 2019), 12–17; James A. Green, *Collective Self-Defence in International Law* (Cambridge: Cambridge University Press, 2024), 76–78, 246–47, 250–54.
[205] Sellars, *'Crimes against Peace'*, 23–28. [206] Mulder, *The Economic Weapon*, 164–75.

doctrine', a decade after the League Covenant had codified the American one, was not lost on contemporary legal experts.[207] For its part, the Japanese government, reassured by Britain's assertion of an interventionist doctrine, embraced the pact as confirmation of the right of self-defence and of 'police action' in its region – a device that was later used to justify its military interventions on the Asian continent.[208]

Moscow's input into Geneva's efforts to define aggression further confirmed the heavily politicized nature of this outlawry of war. Just like the Atlantic victors, the Soviet Union sought to secure itself through universal rules – making total war of conquest a crime, while providing legal cover for continuing and expected communist insurrections in Europe, China, and the colonized world. In the early 1930s Soviet diplomats submitted lists of specific actions that would be defined as aggression, which one British journalist described as 'every excuse ... that any country has ever offered for attacking the Soviet Union'. In the early 1930s Soviet diplomats submitted lists of specific actions that would be defined as aggression, which one British journalist described as 'every excuse ... that any country has ever offered for attacking the Soviet Union'. To provide legal protection for future revolutions, Moscow's list also included domestic conditions that had previously been used by the imperial powers to justify military interventions into the internal affairs of weak states such as 'backwardness', a danger to foreign property and residents and the advent of a new 'political, economic or social order'.[209]

The League's architects did, in fact, want to end the pre-1914 'balance of power' conflicts and arms races that had led to total war, but not simply or even principally by ushering in collective security via disarmament. At its core, the League of Nations was not a pacifist project. It was a critical tool to secure for the Atlantic victors a preponderance of mobilizable military power should it ever be needed, and to minimize the likelihood of that need arising by configuring the global order to inhibit successful great power challenges – goals it accomplished in spades. By its own lights, the League was a near-total security success.

The League Covenant and the security treaties that followed constituted merely the first line of defence, a set of legal-normative barriers to arms races accelerating to total mobilizations. What was called disarmament was in fact arms control; by capping the size of navies, it froze the strategic pecking order of the victors. By far the most important means of 'disarming' the world was the

---

[207] Sellars, *'Crimes against Peace'*, 28–31; J. T. Shotwell, 'A British Monroe Doctrine?' *New York Herald Tribune*, 12 June 1928.
[208] Ian Nish, *Japanese Foreign Policy in the Interwar Period* (New York Praeger, 2002), 62; Hatsue Shinohara, *US International Lawyers in the Interwar Years: A Forgotten Crusade* (Cambridge: Cambridge University Press, 2012), 84–87.
[209] Sellars, *'Crimes against Peace'*, 31–40.

implementation of the Brussels-Genoa Consensus of capitalist globalization premised on gold-backed money, integrated markets, and a small state. In that world the chief victors, the most advanced powers, could deploy high-tech weapons for imperial policing or exercise their control of the oceans and the global economy to threaten sanctions with near-total impunity – thereby protecting themselves from the threat of another global conflagration, and accumulating all sorts of other benefits in the process. And that they now understood all the ways in which a world gearing up for total mobilizations by turning nations into garrison states was inimical to liberal capitalism did not mean that the Atlantic victors did not plan to win a future total war. On the contrary, military staffs in Britain, France, and the United States drew up mobilization plans and legislators passed laws with an eye to quickly converting their countries into giant military-industrial complexes and exploiting fully their collective advantages in natural resources and maritime power.

These war plans and laws assumed that in the unlikely event of another great war erupting, it would emerge in stages, with all the belligerents decoupling from the system of convertible currencies, budgetary balances, world trade, and arms control at roughly the same time. In such a scenario, the Atlantic powers would enter any future great war with both their advantages of the last one and the others that they had acquired since. What actually unfolded in the 1930s was very different. The Great Depression created the conditions for a different kind of competitive arming for total war: one that blurred the legal-normative threshold between peace and war the League had been created to embed. To meet the threat of the Axis of 'have nots', liberal militarism turned to strategies of deterrence in the form of air forces, high-tech frontier fortifications, and naval supremacy.[210] After the threat of League Article 16 failed to deter the Japanese army in 1931 or halt the Italian invasion of Ethiopia in 1935, the Western powers adopted tightening strategies of economic warfare as the fighting in Asia and Europe grew.[211] Nevertheless, in the late 1930s all three Axis challengers ran up against the inferiority in raw materials into which the League-secured order had locked them and from which no programme of autarkic economic development could ever free them. By 1938 the Axis had lost the arms race, and once the war in Europe escalated, the race to total mobilization as well. That Hitler's gamble to escape the growing constellation of economically superior powers arrayed against him paid off in 1939–40 – more out of luck than superior tactics[212] –

---

[210] Joseph A. Maiolo, *Cry Havoc: How the Arms Race Drove the World to War, 1931–1941* (New York: Basic Books, 2011).
[211] Mulder, *The Economic Weapon*, 202–90.
[212] Joseph A. Maiolo, '"To Gamble All on a Single Throw": Neville Chamberlain and the Strategy of the Phoney War', in Christopher Baxter, Michael L. Dockrill, and Keith Hamilton, eds.,

did not alter the fundamental strategic balance.[213] As Mark Harrison has shown, in the total wars of 1914–45 what mattered most was wealth.[214]

In a 1934 lecture Alfred Zimmern argued that, despite appearances to the contrary, the liberal great powers enjoyed an overwhelming preponderance of power over the totalitarian challengers because of their wealth in technology, industry, raw materials, and maritime strength. In that light it is not surprising that the liberal theorist became an early advocate of converting the League of Nations into an alliance of the great democracies.[215] The Palais des Nations did not become the rallying point for that alliance; instead, from 1937, mostly behind the scenes, the transatlantic powers began to reassemble the economic war machine that had won the day in 1917–18. But the principal agents of that coalition were internationally minded military and economic technocrats, some of whom had served in Geneva.[216] These planners were the vanguard of a more militant iteration of transatlantic liberal internationalism: one rooted in the political economy of modern war, determined to crush totalitarian enemies, and inspired by the myth that the League of Nations had been a noble failure.

Epilogue: The Means and Ends of the League of Nations

In the spring of 1946, the nearly defunct League of Nations went on a hiring spree: some two hundred new staff joined the organization by April 1, more than doubling its total numbers. Shortly thereafter, the 21st Assembly (meeting for the first time since December of 1939) officially declared the organization's demise and its replacement with the brand-new United Nations. The League's Secretary General Seán Lester, promoted retroactively from a five-year-long stint in an 'acting' position, wrote to the British civil servant Cecil Kisch: 'You do realise, I know, that our actual work and responsibilities have not been in the slightest degree lessened by the Assembly decision.'[217] Even at this late date, it would seem, the League's operations were far from over.

Britain in Global Politics Volume 1: From Gladstone to Churchill (Basingstoke: Palgrave Macmillan, 2013), 220–41.

[213] Adam Tooze, *The Wages of Destruction: The Making and Breaking of the Nazi Economy* (London: Penguin, 2006).

[214] Mark Harrison, 'Why the Wealthy Won: Economic Mobilization and Economic Development in Two World Wars', in *The Economics of Coercion and Conflict* (Singapore: World Scientific, 2015), 67–98.

[215] Edgerton, *Warfare State*, 55–57.

[216] Thomas Bottelier, '"Not on a Purely Nationalistic Basis": The Internationalism of Allied Coalition Warfare in the Second World War', *European Review of History* 27/1–2 (2020), 152–75.

[217] Victoria Jane Mumby, *The Quiet Death of the League of Nations, 1945–48* (PhD dissertation, Birkbeck, University of London, 2021), 52.

The process of dismantling the League and transferring its pieces to the new United Nations raised many of the same issues that had arisen during its years of regular operation: above all, how to maintain an apparent and visible procedural equity alongside a clearly understood and enforced geopolitical hierarchy, and how to repackage essentially political questions as neutral technical problems to be solved by outside experts. In the event, nearly all of the League's assets and operations – and not a few of its personnel – migrated to the UN, which lived intertwined with the League at the Palais des Nations for the period of the League's dissolution and the UN's construction through 1946 and 1947. During this period the League was evermore loudly decried as a failure, while its operational approach, structural features, material possessions, and political principles came to underpin nearly everything about not only the new organization but the new world order as well.

The Demise of the League

The rumblings of another great war had, of course, already begun to rattle the League some years before its final assembly. The string of diplomatic crises stretching from Japan's conquest of Manchuria to Italy's invasion of Ethiopia, the disarmament talks giving way to arms races, and the outbreak of another European war in the summer of 1939 all appeared to vindicate the League's critics as a naively utopian project lacking teeth. 'The world seemed no different from the way it had been in 1914, or even 1648,' historian Paul Kennedy wrote of the coming of Hitler's war in the summer of 1939. 'The League's final gasp of breath, to expel the Soviet Union for its attack upon Finland that winter, seems more symbolic of its pathos than of its powers. The show was over, and the curtains had closed.'[218]

They hadn't, quite. Throughout this period, the League tried hard to retain its political-diplomatic relevance by doubling down on claims to neutral technical expertise, integrated with American efforts. It began to promote greater cooperation among its technical bodies: in particular, producing a series of conferences and reports on the food crisis that brought the Health Organization into conversation with the ILO, the EFO, the International Institute of Agriculture, and the American Milbank Memorial Fund. The organization's internal structures also came under reconsideration for the purpose of emphasizing its technical bona fides; a proposal to merge the EFO and the ILO, coming in 1938, was touted as producing a 'non-political' body inclusive of American interests and other non-member states. By 1939, the League leadership – now including the voice of

---

[218] Paul Kennedy, *The Parliament of Man: The Past, Present, and Future of the United Nations* (New York: Random House, 2006), 24.

future Australian prime minister Stanley Bruce, appointed to lead a committee on League reform in the aftermath of the invasion of Czechoslovakia – had fully committed to recasting the organization as a series of autonomous technical bodies openly reliant on American funding.[219]

Roosevelt supported this idea politically; the Rockefeller Foundation supported it practically. In February of 1940 the foundation offered to fund the new Economic, Financial and Transit Department – constructed out of the old Economic Intelligence Service – to the tune of $100,000. Arthur Sweetser travelled to the United States in May of 1940 to organize its move across the Atlantic. League Secretary General Joseph Avenol, having briefly pondered moving the League's entire operation to France, abandoned his plans with the fall of Paris in the summer of 1940. After a brief period of turmoil in which he declared that the League had no further options but to 'work hand in hand with Hitler in order to achieve the unity of Europe',[220] Avenol accepted the deal Sweetser had negotiated and resigned. The EFTD would henceforth be located at the Institute for Advanced Studies in Princeton, New Jersey, funded by the Rockefeller Foundation and devoting itself to the study of the 'global economic problems' of population, minorities, migration, monetary policy, and the problems of post-war reconstruction – in other words, all the most central venues for the larger League's long-standing agenda.[221]

The Assembly had already transferred authority to the Secretary General, which was permitted to run a kind of reduced operation out of shrunken offices in Geneva throughout the war, under the supervision of Avenol's successor Lester. Other pieces of the League now also began to drift across the Atlantic. Columbia University Press took over the League's publication service; the Permanent Central Opium Board, the International Narcotics Control Board, and the Advisory Commission on Traffic and Opium all moved to Washington. A proposal to reconstitute the ILO at Johns Hopkins University in Baltimore met with more opposition, not least from Roosevelt himself, and the agency ended up instead occupying a wartime home in Montreal. Major budget cuts to the Secretariat, the League's main remaining political organ, drove home the point that the main energy behind emerging forms of post-war internationalism would henceforth be American – drawing on decades of quiet but meaningful American participation in the League, and a long-standing American

---

[219] See Ekbladh, *Plowshares into Swords*, 89–169, and Tournes, *Philanthropic Foundations at the League of Nations,* 170–72.

[220] Karen Gram-Skjoldager, 'Taming the Bureaucrats: The Supervisory Commission and Political Control of the Secretariat', in Karen Gram-Skjoldager and Haakon A. Ikonomou, eds., *The League of Nations*: *Perspectives from the Present* (Aarhus: Aarhus University Press, 2019), 40–50.

[221] Gram-Skjoldager, 'Taming the Bureaucrats', 178.

commitment to the idea that scientific and technical expertise could defeat political challenges of all kinds in the international realm. After a long process of 'liquidation', the Secretariat finally closed its doors in October of 1947. All the League's assets were moved into new pots at the emerging United Nations.

Wartime Institutions: UNRRA and the IMF

There were other indications of the American-centred, technocratic, economics-driven future of internationalism as well. In November of 1943, the EFTD and the US State Department jointly drafted the charter for a new organization called the United Nations Relief and Rehabilitation Agency (UNRRA), designed to suggest a blueprint for the post-war reconstruction of Europe as a key part of an American-led global economy. 'Being determined that immediately upon the liberation of any area by the armed forces of the United Nations or as a consequence of retreat of the enemy,' UNRRA's founding document declared,

> the population thereof shall receive aid and relief from their sufferings, food, clothing and shelter, aid in the prevention of pestilence and in the recovery of the health of the people, and that preparation and arrangements shall be made for the return of prisoners and exiles to their homes and for assistance in the resumption of urgently needed agricultural and industrial production and the restoration of essential services.[222]

In the event, UNRRA mainly operated as a large-scale refugee agency for the remaining years of the war, running hundreds of camps for 'displaced persons' across Europe, the Middle East, and North Africa and engaging in precisely the same sort of population politics undertaken by the League in the aftermath of the last global conflagration, this time from Washington rather than Geneva.[223] In this work, it relied on the collaboration and participation of the ILO and the League Health Organization, making use of their assets and knowledge; and upon its dissolution in 1948, its operations were transferred to the new International Refugee Organization and the World Health Organization, both of which drew similarly on League precedents. Displacement and resettlement would be key to the remaking of borders, states, and regional orders after this war just as after the last.

Economic institutions, too, were already emerging during wartime as shapers of a post-war global order centred on a highly hierarchical internationalism. At Bretton Woods in 1944, the conceptual and institutional frames for imagining a

---

[222] 'Agreement for United Nations Relief and Rehabilitation Administration', UNRRA S-1536–0000–0009, 9 November 1943, Article I, 2.

[223] Dan Stone, *The Liberation of the Camps: The End of the Holocaust and Its Aftermath* (New Haven: Yale University Press, 2015).

post-war economy shared a basic vision with the League: the establishment of a 'Gold Exchange Standard System', this time based on a dollar convertible to gold; the instantiation of the International Monetary Fund (IMF), which would promote economic stability by issuing short-term loans to stabilize currencies; and the establishment of the International Bank for Reconstruction and Development, intended to provide support for post-war reconstruction. Here, too, the emerging wartime institutions drew on League practice and precedent, particularly with respect to American financial and strategic involvement in developmentalist schemes across the globe.

If many of the League's original practices, from the control of raw materials to the practicalities of mandatory occupation, had emerged from wartime experience, the same was true for the nascent United Nations. Further, though, the kinds of international agencies that sprouted during the Second World War were themselves informed by the League's decades of practice, and in particular by its focus on the bureaucratic, the humanitarian, and the financial as key aspects of global political control. The practice of defining armed conflicts in such a way as to accommodate the strategic and colonial interests of the victors likewise continued in the drafting of the 1949 Geneva Conventions.[224] By the time of the establishment of the United Nations, then, these had been enshrined in both long- and short-term ways as bases of internationalism and strategies for permanent Allied security.

The United Nations and the Legacy of the League of Nations

It has long been recognized, by historians as well as contemporary observers, that the United Nations essentially represented a perpetuation of League practice and theory. 'Although it could never be publicly admitted during or after the war,' Mark Mazower writes in his history of the origins of the UN, 'the truth is that the UN was in many ways a continuation of the earlier body ... It was basically a warmed-up League.'[225] Indeed, the UN that eventually emerged clearly continued the old League's key goals: the production of a system that treated sovereign nation-states with a procedural equity designed to veil an underlying hierarchy of power favouring the old empires and their heirs; and, second, the use of concepts of technocracy, science, and expertise to discredit, override, and render irrelevant the political claims – and political objections – of the masses, inside and outside the imperial metropoles (see Figure 15).

---

[224] Boyd van Dijk, *Preparing for War: The Making of the 1949 Geneva Conventions* (Oxford: Oxford University Press, 2022), and more generally Moyn, *Humane*.
[225] Mazower, *No Enchanted Palace*, 14–15.

Figure 15 The League reimagined: Dong Biwu (front), representative of the Communist Party of China, signing the Charter of the United Nations, San Francisco, 1945. United Nations Photo Library.

The first of these features was immediately evident to any observer of either the League or the United Nations: the structural frame of both paid lip-service to equalities of sovereignty, while explicitly privileging the superpowers of the day as holding special powers and authority. The 'permanent members' of the UN's Security Council clearly paralleled the 'permanent members' of the League Assembly, not to mention the radically disparate forms and degrees of influence wielded by wealthy states at every level of both operations. But it was in its profusion of technical bodies that the UN really made its claim to serve non-political purposes outside – indeed, above – the purview of states, nations, and populations. Today, the UNHCR and UNRWA call themselves 'humanitarian' organizations and declare that they cannot participate in conversations about politics; even as their officials run schools, make decisions about infrastructure, and put into place health care systems, they remain ostensibly 'autonomous from political, economic, military or other objectives'. UNESCO makes crucial decisions on sites, protections, and training based on the recommendations of what it calls its 'expert facility'. The World Bank and the IMF claim the technical capacity to determine who should receive funds and for what purposes. The World Health Organization declares itself a 'team of professionals ... connecting nations, people and partners to scientific evidence they can rely on'. Other examples abound.

This kind of contemporary internationalist reliance on the idea of neutral, scientific, technocratic forms of authority – which can be, and frequently are, deployed to accomplish highly political goals and produce highly specific political outcomes – is a legacy, above all, of the League of Nations. It was at the League that imperial practices were transmuted into 'technical' principles and enshrined in theoretically apolitical structures of authority, with an eye to maintaining imperial-international control over people, territories, and resources irrespective of changing political arrangements. The League's historical importance, then, lies neither in its utopian self-presentation nor in its eventual practical collapse, but in its own quiet but persistent promotion of legalistic procedure, technical knowledge, and regulatory bureaucracy as tools for producing and preserving global inequity. The contemporary world's willing embrace of data-driven 'expertise' as a basis for profoundly consequential policy decisions across the world might well lead us to conclude that the League of Nations, far from being some kind of noble failure, in fact succeeded beyond its founders' wildest dreams.

Acknowledgements

We are grateful, first, to Robert Gerwarth and Michael Watson for their enthusiastic and thoughtful shepherding of this project from its inception. We would also like to thank the many scholars who commented on various aspects of the Element at draft stages: Fiona Adamson, Anthony Best, David Brydan, David Edgerton, Georgios Giannakopoulos, Anne Irfan, Heather Jones, Saho Matsumoto-Best, Jessica Reinisch, Davide Rodogno, Jay Winter, and Vladimir Zubok. We are also very grateful to the Cambridge editorial team and to the Elements in Modern Wars series editors for their help and suggestions. For hosting a workshop about the Element, the authors would like to thank the Sir Michael Howard Centre for the History of War at King's College London. Generous funding for Open Access was provided by the Faculty of Social Science and Public Policy at King's and by Penn State University Libraries Open Publishing. This Element is freely available in an open access edition thanks to TOME (Toward an Open Monograph Ecosystem) – a collaboration of the Association of American Universities, the Association of University Presses, and the Association of Research Libraries – and the generous support of the Pennsylvania State University. Learn more at the TOME website, available at: openmonographs.org.

Modern Wars

General Editor
Robert Gerwarth
University College Dublin

Robert Gerwarth is Professor of Modern History at University College Dublin and Director of UCD's Centre for War Studies. He has published widely on the history of political violence in twentieth-century Europe, including an award-winning history of the aftermath of the Great War, *The Vanquished*, and a critically acclaimed biography of Reinhard Heydrich, the chief organizer of the Holocaust. He is also the general editor of Oxford University Press's *Greater War* series, and, with Jay Winter, general editor of Cambridge University Press's *Studies in the Social and Cultural History of Modern* Warfare series.

Editorial Board
Heather Jones, *University College London*
Rana Mitter, *University of Oxford*
Michelle Moyd, *Michigan State University*
Martin Thomas, *University of Exeter*

About the Series
Focusing on the flourishing field of war studies (broadly defined to include social, cultural and political perspectives), Elements in Modern Wars examine the forms, manifestations, and legacies of violence in global contexts from the mid-nineteenth century to the present day.

Cambridge Elements

Modern Wars

Elements in the Series

The Cultural History of War in the Twentieth Century and After
Jay Winter

Warrior Women: The Cultural Politics of Armed Women, c.1850–1945
Alison S. Fell

Religious Humanitarianism during the World Wars, 1914–1945: Between Atheism and Messianism
Patrick J. Houlihan

The League of Nations
Joseph Maiolo and Laura Robson

A full series listing is available at: www.cambridge.org/EMOW

For EU product safety concerns, contact us at Calle de José Abascal, 56–1°, 28003 Madrid, Spain or eugpsr@cambridge.org.

www.ingramcontent.com/pod-product-compliance
Lightning Source LLC
LaVergne TN
LVHW020332260326
834688LV00037B/1001